The
DAVID HICKS
BOOK OF
FLOWER
ARRANGING

As told to Maureen Gregson

Introduction by Julia Clements

Marshall Cavendish London & New York

To the memory of my father,
who was never without his favourite buttonhole
of a single carnation or a bunch of violets
D.H.

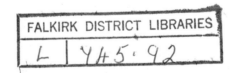
Published by Marshall Cavendish Publications Limited
58 Old Compton Street
London W1V 5PA

© Marshall Cavendish Limited 1976

ISBN 0 85685 171 X

Printed in Great Britain by Jarrold and Sons, Norwich

Other books by David Hicks
David Hicks on Decoration
  Leslie Frewin 1966 (out of print)
David Hicks on Living with Taste
  Leslie Frewin 1968 (out of print)
David Hicks on Bathrooms
  Britwell Books Ltd. 1970
David Hicks on Decoration with Fabrics
  Britwell Books Ltd. 1971
David Hicks on Decoration 5
  Britwell Books Ltd. 1972

Frontispiece: A huge giant hemlock seedhead is all that is needed to add drama to this plain 18th century Welsh dresser, situated in a Dutch country dining room. The simplicity is enhanced by the few pieces of white china placed on the shelves.

Contents

Flower arrangement need not be elaborate or
highly coloured to be effective, as is amply
illustrated by the feathery seedheads I placed
on a high Chinese lacquered stand, against
cola-coloured walls in this London
drawing room.

Introduction

I first met David Hicks in Australia. He was to give a talk on interior design in a Sydney store, but alas, the necessary 'props' had not arrived. Undaunted, to improvise a setting he threw some soft carpets across a few tables with a panache that has now become expected of him. In a few moments the audience had become entranced with all he had to say. Since then, he has produced several books which I loved: now we have *The David Hicks Book of Flower Arranging*.

I have seen many of his flower designs in friends' houses and they are often after my own heart. They always make an impact, a focal point. You do not look at his designs horticulturally – although, of course, they are the end products of horticulture – but you rather accept them as part of the whole interior scheme.

He is certainly original in his approach with flowers: not for him to follow what others have done. Without striving, he does something new each time, on the spur of the moment. I enjoy his colour combinations. When not creating a one-colour scheme, he mixes with aplomb such colours as pale apricot, blackberry, ginger, sharp greens and warm browns, and they always seem right.

Many will enjoy this book for its studied casualness: it proves the use of flowers almost as *objets d'art* in room decoration. Many will recognize their favourite flowers, flowers they grow and use themselves, as well as many more which are not usually seen in arrangement. His taste in flowers is all-embracing, ranging from the humblest wildflower to the grandest lily. A keen gardener, he communicates his own ideas, while keeping an open, flexible attitude to the subject.

When I last saw him, he was leaving for Johannesburg to open his eighth shop and I noticed on a table a vase of clustered, mauve *Iris stylosa*. 'I picked them for you,' he said and, knowing they are considered a connoisseur's flower, I replied, 'I admire your choice.' I wanted to know whether there were any flowers that he dislikes. He answered without any hesitation that he does not like gladioli, bougainvillea and polyantha roses.

A man of decision and action is David Hicks – you can see it in his flower arrangement.

Julia Clements

The pleasure of flowers

To me, one of the great pleasures of flowers is their juxtaposition with furniture, objects, pictures and the general atmosphere of a room. For instance, left, a mass of 'Peace' roses is placed on a white marble topped commode next to a 15th century Buddha's head, in a formalized drawing room arrangement; whereas above, simple honeysuckle is casually grouped with porcelain birds.

Flowers give me more pleasure than almost anything else in life. The colour and smell of them delights me. I love looking at them, growing them, cutting and arranging them and, in this book, I hope to share my personal approach to flower arranging.

My way with flowers has nothing to do with all the traditional rules and regulations which have grown up round the simple idea of bringing fresh flowers and foliage into the house. These restrictions governing the shapes, sizes, colours and ingredients of arrangements developed in more formal times than ours. To my mind, they have little place in today's busier but more casual way of life.

They have also turned an innocently pleasurable pastime into a cult and cults raise barriers. They make people self-conscious and destroy their instinctive enthusiasm.

This book will show that anyone can go out and pick or buy flowers and have the satisfaction of displaying them at home with taste and style – but without difficulty. I want people to relax and take a new look at flower arranging and discover that it can be both easy and fun.

Another myth which should be exploded is that you have to be rich or extravagant to make flower arranging your hobby. Nothing could be further from reality. It is not necessary to buy or grow expensive blooms in order to create a striking composition. Often, a single flower, a seedhead, a clump of hedgerow cuttings or a tiny spring posy in a plain container on a small table, can be infinitely more pleasing than a stiff and intricate display taking up a whole wall.

Among the people who have influenced me, the friends I meet and the clients whose homes I decorate, a natural and unaffected approach to flowers is widespread. All the people I know who handle flowers with great skill and elegance have abandoned the conventions. They go out and experiment and create something quite individual.

For instance, when I paid a September visit to Chateâu de · Mouton, Baroness Philippe de Rothschild arranged a centrepiece for lunch comprising twelve small vases, each containing a different autumnal feature – a Cape gooseberry, a crabtree branch hung with two or three scarlet crab-apples, a head of wild grass, a corn on the cob, an oak branch with acorns, a cluster of hips, a spray of yellow hornbeam leaves, berries and nuts; just autumn prunings to decorate one of the richest tables in France while, outside, the vineyards of the Chateâu stretched for twenty miles.

This epitomized for me what flower arranging is all about. It was basic in concept and uncluttered. None of the seasonal trimmings of the countryside was despised. No flamboyant, hot-house bloom was allowed to break the mood and yet the whole effect glowed with colour and charm. Her arrangements were totally personal.

One of my own favourite ideas is to pack two or three bunches of water-cress into a shallow, square container, sprinkle a little water over the leaves and place it in the centre of the table. It is surprisingly effective. I also use watercress to fill a pair of matching 20cm (8in) *cache pots* on my living room chimneypiece. Inexpensive, simple – and stunning.

Recently, when I opened my new shop in Bayonne, there were none of those bulky florists' concoctions people expect on such occasions. Instead, my associate Christian Badin and I used three white porcelain cylindrical vases of matched design, but of different heights. The tallest contained giant sunflowers, the middle one held smaller sunflowers and the shortest vase was filled with a solid mass of

Above: These vases of different heights and sizes contain giant sunflowers, smaller ones and marigolds.

Below: A charming hanging basket outside a half-timbered cottage in Cheshire, full of typical English country garden flowers.

yellow and brown speckled marigolds. Arranged on a low table, this ravishing build-up of colour drew people to it like a sun.

My love of flowers began in childhood. Although my mother did not arrange them, she was a very good gardener and so I grew up surrounded by plants and blooms. I remember, when I was about sixteen, doing a wildly elaborate autumn arrangement with apples and figs, gourds and berries and yellow and orange flowers and foliage, a crescendo of orangey-red colours at a time when I had certainly never seen anything like it done by anyone else. There was a container, but, by the time I had finished, it had vanished under the harvest extravaganza. Of course, in the exuberance of youth, I had gone too far, but I have never forgotten it and every autumn it is at the back of my mind as I do the flowers at home.

Later, when I was in the Army, I returned home to Suffolk for a short leave and remember going into the garden to pick a bunch of summer flowers, roses, pinks and geraniums. Holding them up to the Constable sky full of puffy, white clouds, I found them so unforgettably beautiful that the same combination of scents can still transport me back in an instant to that day.

After leave and in full uniform, I used to struggle on crowded trains from East Anglia down to the army camp in Kent clutching flowers from the garden, a custom which was considered rather eccentric!

Strangely enough, the person who most influenced my approach to flowers, never tolerated a cut flower in her house. Winnafreda, Countess of Portarlington, was one of the greatest growers of flowers indoors that I have ever met. She did not grow indoor plants. She grew flowers. An Australian, she found the whole English country flower scene hugely exciting when she arrived here before the First World War.

Everything was grown in pots for her home, jasmine, Michaelmas daisies, orchids, pelargoniums, chrysanthemums, everything from spring bulbs and summer annuals to forced winter blooms. Each variety and colour was always massed together. She would have a metre (3ft) wide Korean tub crammed with thirty perfect white cyclamen or a large container planted with white or yellow crocuses, and she taught me more about grouping growing flowers than anyone else I have ever met.

Perhaps it was the sight of her flowers, so strictly collocated by type and colour, which led me to realize later that the excessive complication of traditional methods should be replaced by a cleaner and simpler treatment, so that the arrangements we do retain a certain purity to match the whole movement of modern design or traditional interiors.

Plain blocks of colour, clearly patchworked cushions of flowers, more use of single specimens, more elemental arrangements, less bustle, less paraphernalia, less pretention.

When I look at flowers, plants, foliage and gardens, I question everything. I try to break the mould by providing new sets of answers to old

A build-up of different blues in a simple blue glass vase on a country cottage window-sill.

me, this picking and holding of them in the garden is deeply satisfying. Sometimes that impromptu grouping in the hand cannot be recaptured once you take them indoors, which is very disappointing. It is a good idea, therefore, to stand the container full of water nearby before you start cutting, so that you can put the bunch straight in without laying it down and re-arranging.

Wandering round one's own garden collecting flowers is always absorbing, but nothing is more fun than picking in someone else's garden, though it should be done with care, as it is one way of losing friends.

However, I think of flowers and foliage and arrangements as an ever-expanding, sociable activity, which is always pleasing to do for myself, but even more enjoyable to do for friends.

As soon as I know people are coming to see me, I think of which flowers and vases to use and where to place them. It can take a long time to do the arrangements, but it is very soothing and therapeutic. By the time the friends arrive, I am always relaxed and happy, because it is quite impossible to be otherwise having handled flowers.

It is a pretty thought to do a small individual arrangement for each guest at lunch. This makes a change from the usual centrepiece and most people accept it as an enchanting personal gesture.

Another striking idea is to float flowers. Not only water lilies, but passion flowers and even the individual flowers off a gladiolus stem look exceptional when floated petal to petal in a very shallow container.

As in so many other fields, it is often the unexpected, rather than the ostentatious, which makes the most impact. A bunch of ordinary cottage flowers, dahlias and asters, in reds and pinks, blues and purples, is turned into something special when arranged with reddish beetroot leaves and red and grey cabbage leaves.

Every time you look at a plant you should try to get rid of your pre-conceived ideas about it. Just because you know it as a vegetable is no reason to reject it. The humble cabbage is not only useful for its individual leaves in mixed arrangements, but also as a pot plant.

In America, for instance, red and green ornamental cabbages and kale are grown expressly for the house and are obtainable from many florists;

problems, because, as with my design and decoration work, I am always trying to avoid established habits and *clichés*.

I pick flowers with the vase and setting in mind. The arrangement is casually being composed as I go along. It is not desperately serious, but pleasurable and a little haphazard. The secret is spontaneity, allowing things to happen. Do not always strive for one hard effect as this can result in artificiality, which I do not think suits flowers.

Once you have developed this freer approach, something delicious can take place while you gather the flowers of midsummer. As you put them into the garden basket, they will often position themselves with beautiful naturalness. With the aid of jam jars and shallow bowls for water in the foot of the basket, you can recreate this newly-picked look again indoors. It is an arrangement which is particularly pretty on a hall table near the front door or immediately inside the living room, looking as though someone had just come in from the garden and left the basket there.

It takes half an hour or so to gather the flowers for just one vase and, for

On a circular, marble-topped French metal
table of the early 19th century, a group of
almost totally dissimilar objects from
many countries are related only by their
colour. I sometimes place a single bloom of
a completely contrasting colour among
them, in this instance, a yellow water-lily
in a small blue glass vase. The small
picture on an easel is by Peter Upward.

and, in China, cabbages are planted ornamentally in geometric patterns and look most intriguing.

Other plants which are usually overlooked may also have a grace all their own, as with a clump of dried dock seed heads or a cushion of parsley in a circular or square container under a spotlight. Town dwellers may find an astonishing collection of long grasses and attractive weeds in wild corners of parks and commons, or on the roadside verges while out for a weekend family drive. All may be used later, fresh or dried, at home.

What matters is the *arrangement* and the arrangement of inexpensive things is just as important as the arrangement of expensive ones, whether we are talking of plants, objects, or paintings.

One of the most fascinating aspects of this subject is that the same arrangement never, ever occurs twice. There is always an unending number of variations to be made on one theme. If you take the combination of a particular vase and perhaps three or four different types of flowers – carnations, lilies, sweet peas and London pride (*Saxifraga umbrosa*) – over and over again, you will always have different results. This gives an enthralling depth to flowers.

Late every June I pick fifty Peace roses of exactly the same length of stem and cram them into a very large bowl. They are almost identical year after year, although they are not the same as those on page 6, which were picked in September, when the rose is smaller and a different colour from the blooms of the first flush.

However, although I do this arrangement annually, I do not allow it to become stale. To give variety, I use different vases and also different positions in the house.

People tend to have one place in their living room where they always put the flowers and which is never altered. Habits like this ought to be broken, because they lead to dullness. I am always changing the positions of the objects, sculptures and flowers at home, striving to find new places and ideas to give different effects and continual interest to the eye.

Another mistake many people make in their approach to flowers is to think that an arrangement must last. Yet I often use blooms which only last for a single day, or even a few hours. Nothing could be prettier on a summer lunch table than to have eight single ipomoeas in small containers (eggcups are excellent) round a china vase full of flowers. Another marvellous bloom, which must be picked after it has opened to the sun and which will only last some hours, is the brilliant orange-yellow flower of the ordinary vegetable marrow. It is worth the effort just for its extraordinary effect.

You cannot have too many flowers in a house, but this does depend on how they are handled and placed. A surfeit of formal vases will turn a room into a funeral parlour, while too many heavy, sensual flowers can be suffocating. The answer lies again in diversity. You need tall displays, low posies, medium conventional arrangements, mixed flowers, single specimens and then perhaps containers of foliage.

A splendidly architectural ornamental cabbage like this is a superb thing on its own, growing in a pot or placed in a container, and I do not despise single leaves for use in other arrangements.

When I visited Rathbeale Hall, Co. Dublin recently, there must have been twenty flower arrangements in the drawing room alone, but, apart from one or two quite large compositions, most were small, a little vase of roses, a glass with two lilies, many tiny nosegays. The effect was personal and very feminine.

I do believe that, on the whole, men and women arrange flowers differently and, although I have discarded the formal traditions, this does not include those big romantic arrangements which some women do exquisitely. Delicately coloured peonies and roses blended with softly arching branches of blossom, such as escallonia or choisya are deliciously evocative.

With these kinds of arrangements, the person I admire very much indeed is the Duchess of Buccleuch, who has the most hauntingly fragile way with flowers I have ever seen.

Those men who are passionately interested in flowers tend to treat them with great boldness and drama. It is probably true to say that the creation of colour effects and build-ups with flowers generally means more to me than their architecture. This is why I am, personally, less interested in deliberate arrangements revolving round the shape of individual plants and flowers, than in massed colour and grouping.

It is the individual approach which is so fascinating. Just as no arrangement can ever truly be repeated, so no two people display flowers in the same way. I think the way a person arranges flowers does very much reflect his or her personality. There are even people who never have flowers or plants in their homes at all and I always imagine they must be lazy, insensitive or mean, because even annuals can be grown in pots and a packet of seed costs very little.

The point of using plants and flowers indoors is to give the home personality and life, and it is really important to find the flowers and leaves which suit your room. I hope, through the illustrations in this book, to demonstrate how this is done, because it is a very subtle business which cannot accurately be spelt out in words. First, you have to recognize it in photographs, paintings and in other people's methods; then you must experiment and practise until, suddenly, one day you will discover that you have achieved it, your own, individual unique style with flowers.

Above: An utterly simple vase with a random collection of typical country garden flowers and foliage.

Below: One spray of magnificent lilies like this placed in a simple cylinder can be infinitely more enjoyable and dramatic than an arrangement of four or five.

Flowers and plants for colour and style

You can do so much with colour, using both flowers and foliage. Daring combinations, such as common orange marigolds (left) in a room with geranium pink felt walls and an Etruscan red sofa set up an exciting vibration of colour. Above, a group of mauve and scarlet anemones with raspberry pink dianthus make a focus of colour on a snake-skin covered table, in front of a Graham Sutherland gouache.

The first thing to be said about colour is that clashing colours do not exist. The whole idea of certain colours conflicting violently with others was a nonsense dreamed up by a lot of genteel women in the nineteen-thirties. Colours do not clash – they vibrate.

Too much time is spent, too much rubbish talked, too many rules adhered to and endless energy put into deciding which colour will go with which and, as a result of this, most people are afraid of the whole subject. Yet there is no reason why they should be, because there are really very few colours which do not go together.

Colour means more to me in every aspect of my work than any other raw material. I am constantly enthralled by experimenting with it and exploiting it, and I know that it is one of the most stimulating and rewarding and inexpensive pleasures in life and in this book I hope to pass on some of my enthusiasm.

Some guiding lines applicable to both decoration and flower arranging were evolved by designers and decorators in the immediate post-war period. All reds go together, all pinks go together, just as it has always been accepted that all blues and all yellows do. All reds, pinks, yellows and oranges will mix and so will all mauves and blues. All greens, being the basis of plant life, mix with each other and with all flowers.

Although convention is the main root of the confusion on this subject, it is absolutely true that certain colours do vibrate when they are used together, but there is nothing wrong with this. It is exciting and I use such mixtures to make dull corners sizzle. For instance, in a room mostly containing beiges, browns and yellows, I would add a shocking pink and orange flower arrangement, such as pink camellias and tangerine azaleas.

So, do not be afraid to use colour freely. Have courage. As with drawing, painting, acting or any creative activity, you must attack with strength.

You must also learn how to make the most impact with your materials, because, although virtually all colours mix, they are best used to build up to specific colour effects.

People are so inclined to get one red lamp or a couple of blue cushions and then relate them to nothing else. But, just as you have to co-ordinate your decorating with the curtain fabric, the carpet and the furniture, so the same type of relationship must be

discovered with flowers. While arranging them, you should be working out their pleasing contrasts of texture, shape and, above all, colour.

I think I probably originated the use of flowers to make blocks of colour, taking six pink and eight white carnations and a dozen lavender phlox and using them in blocks, instead of intermingled as arrangers had done previously.

A vase containing twelve cream roses, six deep yellow and six orange ones arranged in chromatic masses has far more dominance than, say, six pink, six yellow, six white and six red all muddled in together. Another good composition for roses at the height of the season is twelve vibrant pink, six apricot and six flame; at the same time, two dozen matched blooms of the same colour always look marvellous.

Broadly speaking, flower arrangements should be related to the entire background in which they are placed. However, the colour statement may be built up in only one section of the room; on the chimneypiece, in a corner, or on a table.

Perhaps the table theme is to be white. This may be achieved through one or two pieces of white china, a table lamp with white shade and white porcelain base and an onyx *objet d'art*. To these could be added the finishing touch of a white pottery cylinder vase full of white Shasta daisies.

On the other hand, I have a rather plain table which always needs the multicoloured sparkle of a little vase of anemones, or asters, or ranunculus. Another, larger table is more suited by an architectural composition of fennel, cow parsley or hosta leaves.

Generally, muted colours should be used to contrast with bright objects, but, as I believe all rules are made to be broken, you will see in the illustration on page 14, that I have put a large bowl of brilliant orange marigolds in a room full of vibrant colours, where it looks splendid. This is because that room is such an incredible combination of dazzling mauves, magentas and lacquer reds that a delicate, pale arrangement would be completely overpowered.

I have another room in London where I also break the reverse rule that vivid colour should be used to contrast with muted surroundings. This living room has cream walls and cream curtains. The colour there is very subtle indeed and, were I to plunge in

I believe in colour build-up, and on the facing page are many ordinary garden or bought flowers which can achieve this effect. In the top row you will see yellows which I would put together, interspersed to achieve extra drama by having 'yellow on yellow on yellow'. Shown here, left to right, are Lilium pyrenaicum (tiger lily) Reinwardtia trigyna and Rosa 'Courvoisier' (a floribunda). In the second row you will see how marigolds (Calendula officinalis) roses (Rosa 'Southampton'), and nasturtiums (Tropaeolum majus) in varying shades of orange and yellow, may be mixed together with great effect. The third row down shows ranunculus, tulips (Tulipa darwinii 'London') and a strident hybrid tea rose ('Super Star') which can all be used effectively in a conglomeration, either interspersed with each other or arranged in blocks of each variety. In the bottom row I have shown a modern hybrid tea rose ('Shannon'), a single dianthus (Dianthus neglectus) and a bourbon rose ('Louise Odier'), which would all combine very effectively together in a midsummer arrangement.

In my house in the south of France, I
have a permanent arrangement of dried
gypsophila in a simple white pottery
cylinder. I usually place it on this steel,
glass-topped table which has a
'tablescape' of rock crystal, calcite (or
Iceland spar), two pieces of sculptured
Orefors glass, three simple white plastic
boxes and a single datura, a super plant
which of course, needs a Mediterranean
heat for it to bloom.

with dazzling flowers, the impact would be far too violent.

The flowers which look good there are cream or very pale yellow roses, or pink lilies and white blooms. Daffodils look well there, but they have to be the cream ones rather than the yellow.

It is, in some ways, a severe interior with stark furniture and a contrast is needed, a change of pace, a change of gear. One of my favourite effects is achieved with a bouquet of dried gypsophila in a stainless steel cylindrical vase. In America, this plant is called baby's breath and indeed it does have an etherial quality – it floats in a soft *pointilliste* manner. It provides a necessary softness and textural interest, without which the room would seem terribly bald and cold. It partly covers the mirror over the chimneypiece and is well related through contrast to its steel vase.

If, however, the room had white, as opposed to cream walls, then the stronger the colour the better. A vase of massed sizzling blue cornflowers looks wonderful in a white room.

The transformations which can be achieved through the simple use of colour through flowers are quite astonishing. The corals, reds and orangey-pinks of poppies, geraniums and Super Star roses will warm up the coldest room, and a bleak, north-facing room will be infinitely more welcoming with a splash of glowing sunflower yellow.

A dingy basement can be brightened with burnished orange calendulas, or zinnias, or a large pot of rambling nasturtiums. In hot summer, accents of brilliant yellows, oranges or pinks, or clear yellows used with transluscent greens will bring freshness to sunlit rooms. Blue is a very cool colour.

Dark colours are warming and the sharp days of late autumn are right for huge copper chrysanthemums, plum, wine and purple tones and rich evergreens.

The one colour rarely thought about in flowers is green, which most people associate with leaves only. Yet green flower arrangements have a delicacy which manages to produce a different aura for each season: lightness in winter, freshness in spring, coolness in summer and a certain nostalgia in autumn. Lime blossom, bells of Ireland (*Molucella laevis*), sea holly (*Eryngium*), ornamental hops (*Humulus lupulus*), nicotiana, the Corsican hellebore (*Helleborus corsicus*), the old-fashioned

Above: Sea holly (Eryngium) has a wonderfully cool and architectural quality for hot summer days.

Below: An interesting, early 19th century, salt glaze jug holds an enchantingly pastoral bunch of herbs and hedgerow gatherings.

Shades of white, cream and ivory have
a cool, uncluttered effect in this room
with murals by Rex Whistler. On a
circular galleried table I placed an
inexpensive bunch of Shasta daisies in a
white vase, amid a collection of white
Chinese porcelains and under a white
'bisquit' bust of Marie Antoinette, given to
Lady Palmerston by the Empress Eugenie.

rose 'Madame Hardy', Norway maple blossom, daphne, lady's mantle (*Alchemilla mollis*), *Garrya elliptica* and wild parsley all produce green flowers at different times of the year. Used with other colours, they tend to become lost amongst the foliage, but used alone or with each other, their individual shades and shapes show up very well.

It is the successful use of colour which gives style. The concentration of all sorts of yellows, greens and oranges, the putting together of blues, purples and reds, the explosive effect on the eye of a splash of one startling colour in an otherwise uneventful place make style. And style is what this whole book is really about.

Just as notes played together in the right way become music for our pleasure, so the harmonious mingling of materials and colours also delights our senses. A tasteless combination will offend the eye as much as a wrong note jars the ear.

Of course, the Japanese have taken style to a very highly developed cult in Ikebana, their form of flower arranging, but I find it too contrived. While these arrangements are superb in traditional Japanese rooms, I do not think they have a place in Europe, any more than a classic Constance Spry arrangement would look right in Japan.

To me, flowers are sensual enchantment, rather than spiritual, and Ikebana, with its concern for higher planes and hidden meanings is altogether too intellectual for my own attitude towards flower arranging.

Style produces atmosphere and, if the atmosphere is right, then the arrangement has taste. People can be born with taste, or they can acquire it, providing they are aware of what it is. It is a gradual development of visual awareness. It is a matter of being interested in all you see and use, and of continually searching, selecting and experimenting.

I do not think taste can be taught, but I think it can be learnt. It is a question of using the eye and endlessly pruning and disciplining and thinking.

One of the secrets of style is that, whether you decide to do an arrangement, or a design, or anything else, you must do it boldly and not dither.

Again and again, it is not so much the material you use, as the way that you use it. Decide the approach you are going to take and the impression you wish to create, then do it with love, with conviction, with a sense of scale and a sense of contrast, and with luxury.

By luxury, I do not mean expense. A clump of grasses looks luxurious if it is big enough. The matching vases of watercress I am so fond of using at home look luxurious. A dozen garden pinks will look sparse and leggy if left loosely on long stems in a vase. Cut the stems down and push them into a smaller container, so that the flowers mass together in a cushion, and you have – luxury.

Almost any flower benefits from being cut short and stuffed into a vase so that all the blooms are close to each other and give the maximum impact, but this is totally contrary to most people's idea of what to do with them.

Taste is in no way dependent on money. I detest gladioli in expensive cut-glass vases. They have the minimum of effect for the maximum of expense. Instead, I prefer a wide basket tightly packed with marguerites – a maximum effect for the minimum expense.

When planning your flowers, you not only have to think of the decoration and the objects and furniture in your room, you should also think of the flowers in relation to where you sit and stand. This is the aspect of flower positioning most frequently overlooked and yet it is very important and can sometimes mean the difference between the success or failure of your efforts.

Arrangements do not always have to be stood on a table or chimney shelf. A galvanized bucket (which, incidentally, makes an excellent flower container) full of towering giant hogweed, or mighty wild rhubarb leaves, standing on the floor will look particularly good from an armchair. The foliage will tower above you as it was designed to do by nature.

'Cushion' arrangements are often especially successful when placed on low tables so that the mass of flower heads is always seen from above, and arrangements of scented flowers or foliage should always be placed reasonably low, so that their scent can pervade the room and they can be easily touched and smelt by everyone. Never put them out of reach on a high fireplace, as their scent will only rise further with the warm air to hang under the ceiling and be wasted.

Although I confess to the deepest interest in colour, I also enjoy plants as architectural features. Yuccas, for example, are marvellous. The knife-

Although giant hogweed, even before it becomes dried has little colour, the build-up of beiges and similar colours is just as important as the vibrations created by brilliant pinks and oranges. These seed-heads have great grandeur, and should be placed where their height can be seen to advantage, such as in this simply furnished dining room.

The inter-relation of lamps with pictures and arrangements of objects on table tops and chimneypieces is not only important but great fun to play with. Sometimes it is nice to have objects fitting neatly together, so that one does not overpower another, but on other occasions I relish unorthodox juxtapositions.

like leaves can be used very creatively in arrangements and, when the bloom is cut, it should be featured alone, stood absolutely upright in a solid, cylindrical vase.

I also use bamboos, ferns, bull-rushes, dried flowers, and in winter, great branches of Scots pine architecturally. However, such plants and leaves are only good if they are used on a really terrific scale. It does not matter how small or low your room, you can still put the vase on the floor with a huge display against the wall and make an impressive element. Never be afraid of scale. When you are arranging spring blossom, or winter cherry, do not just cut little sprigs. Cut really good great big branches and have a lovely, generous arrangement that fills the room.

Relating flowers to the proportions of their immediate settings and the objects around them is not as difficult as it may sound, although some people have the knack instinctively and others have to acquire it.

To return to the side table; it may have a lamp on it and a picture on the wall behind it. There may also be an ashtray and an object. The flower arrangement will obviously need to fit comfortably below the lampshade and yet, to make any impression beneath the painting, it must not be too contained. A small bunch of violets will be outshone and a branch of blossom will obscure the light and detract from the picture. So the answer must lie somewhere between the two. It is a delicate balance of taste.

Fireplaces are always useful for flower arrangements and pairs of vases usually look good there. It is not always necessary to aim for the symmetry of having one at each end of the chimneypiece. They may be placed together, slightly to the right or left of centre, or at one end where, in certain circumstances, they may look more striking.

With my twin vases, I often like to do pairs of arrangements, filling each vase with very similar contents. However, I do not attempt to make them absolutely identical. It is never a good idea to have flowers too regimented. The two compositions are not intended to be exact reflections of each other, but rather two different versions of the same flower combinations.

Because the fireplace is the focal point of most rooms, it is the place where, in the off season, I like to see just one early tulip, or three winter

aconites, or the first snowdrops: mixed up in the clutter of the chimney-piece, this can have great charm.

Apart from using twin vases, I enjoy putting related vases together. These either contain related arrangements, or they are of identical design, but different sizes. The sunflower and marigolds that I referred to in the first chapter are a good example of this. The three vases used varied only in height and the flowers interacted through the build-up of their colours.

Late last summer I did another variation of this, with a very early rust, orange and yellow foretaste of autumn in a large container and, in a smaller vase just in front of that, light pink, scarlet and white geranium buds, together with a few very small pink rosebuds and three late pale-pink lilies. The last breath of summer overshadowed by the heralds of the new season.

Along with colour, scale and contrast, texture is also an important ingredient of our style and one which people usually only explore superficially, perhaps because we barely notice our sense of touch. Yet tactile objects are intriguing.

The texture of flowers, foliage and fruit is an essential, though often underrated part of their appeal to us. Think of the roughness of Fir-cones, the polished smoothness of the leaves of *Magnolia delavyi*, the feathered softness of ferns, the downy skin of the peach and the damp velvet of rose petals, all of which add to their beauty.

At home, I try to exploit this by placing on tables and sometimes on the floor, pots and containers filled with natural, touchable contents, often derived from plants. Dried rose petals, sandalwood shavings which are heavily scented, lavender seeds, shells and coloured stones from the seashore, dried leaves of the scented geraniums, sunflower seeds; anything in fact, which looks good and invites touch, so that people are drawn to sift the contents through their fingers and play with them. Children, especially, love these, but people of all ages are also attracted to them.

Fresh flowers, plants and leaves can also interplay with them. Newly cut lavender may be placed next to the bowl of lavender seeds, or the colour of the faded rose petals picked up in a soft lilac and pink posy, or the speckled beige, pink, mauve and green tones of the beach stones carried into an arrangement of sea holly

(*Eryngium*), sweet peas and stocks.

There are so many ways of arranging flowers. There are small, slim vases for single blooms, and specimen vases, like that in the illustration on page 37 for displaying together one of each of several varieties. These are especially useful in late autumn, winter or early spring, when there are so few flowers around.

You can have a completely mixed bouquet, or a disciplined bunch of only one variety and one colour, or of several varieties sharing the same colour. You may use your flowers like a painter's palette to build up colour themes.

A bunch of roses, a bunch of gypsophila and daphne, Canterbury bells and acanthus can be grouped in one vase, or in separate vases of different heights placed close together. Clippings, prunings, roadside weeds and grasses provide a wealth of material you may not have used before.

So there is no need to return to starchy old traditions, with flowers sticking out of vases in all directions like bicycle wheel spokes, nor should we ever have to fall into lazy habits and *clichés* through lack of inspiration.

If you have always put that same vase of daffodils in that same corner every spring, do something different! If the dried flowers in the hall have long since turned into dead flowers encrusted with dust, either throw them out and start again, or rearrange them and put them in a new place.

Above all, start thinking. Plan to use new materials and adopt new methods and look with new eyes. Then you will suddenly hear your family and friends genuinely commenting on the flowers, instead of just murmuring polite courtesies or, worse still, not even seeing them. They may be impressed, surprised, or even disapproving of your new arrangements, but they will certainly *notice*.

You can buy pot pourri or you can make it up yourself, and you can use it in many different containers open or closed. This picture shows many-coloured pot pourri in a Victorian brown glazed bowl with a serrated edge.

Cutting and care for arrangement

Cut flowers need care before arranging them, but after that, I have a flexible attitude. Left, beautiful old-fashioned roses and peonies are off-set by a surprising mop-head hydrangea, while above, simple hosta flowers work with cool jade, pottery and marble objects, including Chinese jade archery thumb pieces.

Going out to pick flowers on a summer morning, before the rest of the household is really awake, is one of my favourite ways of starting the day. The flowers are covered in dew and this is, in fact, the very best time to pick them, because they have had the long, cool night in which to revive after the warmth of the day before.

They may also be picked in late evening, but the one time you should not gather flowers is at the height of the day, when they are limp from having lost much of their moisture to the sun.

Never, ever pull, or break flowers by hand, as this bruises and damages the stems badly. The only exceptions to this are cyclamen and *Iris stylosa*, each flower of which must be pulled out from the base, as any remnant of stem tends to develop mould which eventually rots the whole plant.

It is worth making little preparations before you go into the garden. If you are lucky enough to have a utility room, or scullery with a sink, try to keep it as a flower room. Probably you will have to share it with the children's Wellington boots and all manner of garden implements, as I do. But you can store your vases and containers on shelves around it and keep all your arranging equipment ready in a cupboard there.

Most people, however, have to arrange their flowers in the kitchen and the secret there is to make sure there is plenty of surface space. So, clear away first!

Basic requirements for the garden are a good pair of secateurs for woody stalks and a pair of sharp scissors for flower stems. Some flower arrangers prefer to use a pruning knife which they maintain gives a cleaner cut and causes less damage, but using one of these does require some practice and I am convinced that there is not much difference between the two methods.

All stems should, however, be cut at an angle, in the same way as roses are pruned, and perennials must have sufficient leaves left at the base to ensure that the plant lives on after the flowers have been cut. It is not a good idea to cut a perennial too hard. Always leave some blooms growing, if you want the plant to come up again next year. Carnations should be cut at an angle between the joints.

If you intend to arrange the flowers immediately and have no time to condition them beforehand, it is good to leave a bucket of water in a shaded corner of the garden so that the flowers can be placed straight in water as they are cut. Rain water is best for all plants if you have a water butt. In cold weather, the water should have the chill taken off it as the shock of being plunged into icy water does not do the living plant any good.

I must confess that I do not often follow this routine myself, because, to me, one of the delights of gathering flowers is the way they group together in my hand or in the basket, so often forming a natural arrangement there, which I immediately transfer into the vase if I can.

However, when one of my arrangements is required to last for as long as possible, I do follow the rules of conditioning.

The first of these is that each flower must be picked at the right stage of its life cycle; too early and it will not develop properly, too late and it will die too soon.

Everyone knows that there is not much point in cutting a full-blown rose, as the petals will fall before it reaches the vase, but many people are unaware of the best times to pick other flower varieties.

Mimosa is the only flower which should be fully developed and covered with pollen. This is why it does not last long and needs the greatest care. The stems should be placed for thirty seconds in three inches of boiling water and, once arranged, the flowers should be sprayed regularly with cool water to prolong their lives.

Mimosa is, of course, exceptional. Usually, pollen indicates that the flower is past its best. This particularly applies to Michaelmas daisies, rudbeckia, dahlias, tickseed (*Coreopsis*), arcotis and marguerites. These should be cut while their centres are still firm.

Chrysanthemums should be in full bloom before being cut. Poppies should be cut just as their buds are bursting open and the petals showing, and peonies as soon as their petals begin to open. Hydrangeas should be cut on new wood only. Blossom should always be cut when the buds are very tight, as should the budding branches of trees, such as horse chestnut, alder and willow, so that they can open beautifully in the warmth of the house.

Although my arrangements are not planned in advance, on reaching the garden I automatically start thinking of how the flowers will be used as I gather them. I visualize the salmon pink rose

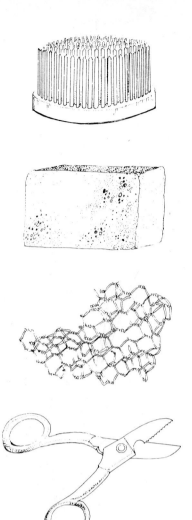

Above: Some of the acceptable aids to arrangement. Top to bottom, a pinholder to be used in conjunction with wet sand or newspaper; absorbent plastic foam; chicken wire; flower scissors.

Right: This giant fennel was cut in summer when green and stood in a massed group in a large glass container, beside an Athenian carving mounted on a stand. Lit from above by a strip light over the painting, I allowed it to dry naturally in the vase so that in winter it still looked very well.

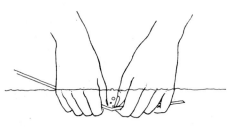

Above: To avoid an air-lock, break stems under water. Dahlias, peonies and stocks benefit from this treatment.

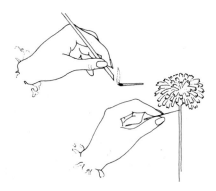

Above: For stems that 'bleed', seal them immediately after cutting by applying a lighted taper to the stem ends. To prevent an air-lock forming, prick the stem with a pin below the flower head.

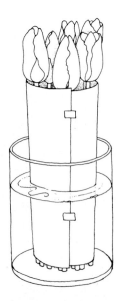

Above: Tulips can be stiffened by supporting them in a chimney of stiff paper in water, before finally arranging them.

in contrast to a strident blue-pink geranium, or the sugar pink hollyhock with the apricot Californian poppy (*Eschscholzia*).

Even for the longest lasting arrangements, I do not necessarily discard imperfect flowers. Occasionally, I may pick a rather weedy-looking rose, because perhaps it is the only one with just the right note of bright red to go with a shocking pink bloom in the vase, and the removal of a crumpled petal or two will leave it looking quite acceptable.

As I pick, I am not only thinking about colour and shape, but also about the height of the prospective arrangement. Sometimes, a bunch of flowers all exactly the same height looks very interesting.

Although you should not cut perennials too hard, you must still be bold when cutting other flowers and leaves. Most people, in their anxiety to have flowers in the house and in the garden, finish up with too little in both, which is useless.

When I find a great patch of flowers or foliage, I pick heaps of them. If you are going to do an arrangement of docks, for example, you need masses of them to look good. You can see what I mean in the illustration of the fennel display on page 27. One or two stalks of fennel would have looked nondescript, but I picked almost the whole patch and the effect was stunning, visually, texturally and for the smell, which filled the room. Later, this arrangement dried out naturally and its seedheads are now in a number of my dried flower arrangements at home.

It is in order to be able to create effects like this that I rarely follow the gardeners' rule of lifting and dividing perennials. I want to find over-generous clumps of blooms every year, so that there are plenty for both house and garden.

Your flowers will live longer if they are left in deep water for several hours before being arranged, but different plants require different treatment.

Flowering shrubs, roses, lilac and similarly woody-stemmed plants should have the ends of their stalks lightly crushed with a hammer, or you can make a couple of one inch splits up the stems.

Chrysanthemums also require this treatment and they then respond well to being left for about four hours in warm water. In fact, next to orchids, they are the longest lasting flowers.

Carnations, too, benefit from a drink of warm water after cutting.

Dahlias, peonies, stocks and most foliage should be given a long drink of quite hot water. Many people break off their stems again under water, in case an air-lock has formed which will stop the flowers drawing in water.

Certain flowers last better after having been completely immersed in water, (including their blooms) for a while. These are florist-bought roses, camellias, gardenias and pansies. The last three should be handled as little as possible, as they are easily bruised. Violets, too, react well to being floated in lukewarm water for an hour.

Wilted flowers, even blossom, can often be revived by recutting the stems and dipping the ends in boiling water for about half a minute, then plunging into deep, warm water for about three hours.

There are flower stems which 'bleed' after they have been cut. These include poppies, dahlias, tulips, Christmas roses and some other plants. They should be sealed immediately by applying a flame to the ends of their stems, or by dipping them into boiling water for thirty seconds. They should be pricked just below the flowerhead with a pin, to release any air-lock and help preserve their straightness, and then stood in a bucket full of water.

To most people tulips are the most maddening flowers to arrange. No sooner are they in position than they droop. This can be very attractive by accident, but it may not have been your intention at all.

If the tulip stems are wrapped so that they are firmly supported up to the heads in a 'chimney' of stiff, non-absorbent paper during their first long drink in deep water, this does stiffen them and help to keep their stance. It is also said that if they are placed so that they can 'see' their reflections in a mirror, they straighten up. But I do not guarantee that!

Bulb flowers like daffodils, narcissi, hyacinths and tulips, cannot absorb water through the white end of the stem, so this must be cut back to where the stem is all green, and the thick juice they exude should be washed away under a tap.

One of the problems with a long-lasting arrangement is keeping the water sweet. Of course, all unnecessary foliage below the water line should have been removed from the flower stems as soon as possible after cutting

Although many of my arrangements comprise flower heads cushioned tightly together in rather squat containers, foliage acts as the anchor for my larger displays. I start by putting the foliage in place, so that I can then pin everything else down by its sheer weight and, in seasons when flowers are scarce, I simply use extra branches of evergreens. Occasionally, I do an entire composition of different kinds of foliage and integrate just one late bloom. This is a splendid way to display a perfect flower or stunning colour.

Because of this method, I personally do not use aids to flower arranging. I am lucky enough to live in the country and can always cut more foliage from the garden when necessary.

However, there are many aids available to the town dweller. Most of these are more useful than attractive, but one or two are both practical and intrinsically pretty.

My favourite aids are the little Victorian glass flower holders. These are ornamental in their own right and can still be found in junk shops, where they are often cheaper than their ugly modern counterparts.

Another charming Victorian flower object is the hyacinth bulb glass, which was used to grow a single hyacinth with water only. Modern bulb glasses are usually well designed and it is an intriguing way to grow this flower indoors.

If I have to give support to a single flower, or a group of two or three specimens, I prefer to use damp sand, which holds both the stems and the water they need. There are several other proprietary aids to arrangement (see page 26), but as I always like flowers to look natural, I avoid most of these products on the whole. This also goes for florists' wire, as I never wire flowers under any circumstance.

If you are unable to obtain enough foliage for your arrangement and do find it necessary to support the blooms artificially, avoid creating a mannered impression. In such a situation, I would prefer to cut my flowers shorter and display them in a smaller container, because, by holding flowers at impossible angles, artificial aids often destroy the elemental effect we should try to create.

The 'look' I always aim for is an artless balance, with flowers and branches relating to each other freely, building up a harmonious design.

Garden flowers, herbs, wild flowers and foliage are placed in the vase much as they were gathered, making a delightfully natural arrangement. 'Tired' marigolds and other thin stemmed flowers can be revived by recutting and resting them in warm water for a while.

otherwise they can make the water unpleasant.

There are one or two reliable products available from florists for keeping the water pure, but one of the best methods is to leave a small piece of charcoal in the foot of the vase. Some people add an aspirin, or leave copper in the water, or add a couple of drops (no more) of disinfectant, or detergent, or a teaspoonful of salt to the container.

Delphiniums, lupins, daffodils, narcissus and larkspur last a little longer if about a dessertspoonful of sugar is added to their water.

Several flower species open at dawn and close at dusk, water lilies and marrow flowers being two good examples. A drop of molten wax placed at the base of the petals will keep them open in your arrangement, and wax will also help open tulips, chrysanthemums and dahlias, and it will help a number of other flowers to retain their petals longer.

Using vases and containers

Containers are important to the whole effect of flower arrangement, though they do not have to be expensive. Opposite, an ordinary wastepaper basket holds masses of ripe wheat, on a Ghanaian tablecloth; whereas above, a delicately coloured, early 19th century, French chinoiserie vase suits a late summer cottage garden arrangement.

Most people think of vases and containers as being special and expensive, but, if they only looked round their kitchen, cellar, attic or garden shed, they would find all sorts of useful receptacles for holding plants and flowers. The most ordinary, everyday objects can make the best containers.

Basically, I think that containers should be simple and not too highly coloured, though these are guides rather than hard and fast rules.

The main point of a vase is to show off your flowers to their best advantage and, therefore, I prefer to use absolutely plain glass, pottery or china cylinders, cubes, rectangles, oblongs and ovals.

Nevertheless, there are obviously a lot of antique, romantic, shaped vases which can look extremely pretty. These are clearly more suitable for a country cottage sitting room or a country house drawing room than for a town apartment. In a modern office, for example, nothing would look more incongruous than a highly coloured, early 19th century, flower-covered, gilded vase.

However, the converse is not true, because I would use on an elaborate period piece of furniture, perhaps next to an ornate period lamp, a very simple, stainless steel cylinder – and the disparity would be pleasing.

Apart from the occasional beautiful old vase, almost anything can be used as a container. The most unlikely objects may be revealed as excellent flower vases, provided you keep in mind that they must have clean, straight lines, because these make the right contrast to the flowers and leaves spilling out over them.

So, in the kitchen, you will discover that coffee jars, round and square-shaped, are ideal; the large ones for holding spring and summer bouquets and the smaller ones for posies. Octagonal jam jars and some of the prettier glass honeypots make good containers for bunches of such flowers as anemones, candytuft, coreopsis and zinnia – flowers which can be cut short and made into a cushion, or a little handful of creamy Christmas roses, or spring fritillaria, or winter irises.

I put two or three sky-blue ipomoea, or golden hypericum, or pansies, in a small cylindrical container at each place setting at lunch parties.

A white, china *soufflé* dish makes a splendid container and, in spring, I either pick, or dig up an immense bunch of primroses and put them tightly into such a dish. The advantage of digging them up is that the flowers last longer indoors and, when they die back, the plant can be replaced, undamaged, in the garden.

One of my favourite ways of displaying very large concentrations of wild flowers, grasses, foliage or grain such as wheat, corn or barley, is to cram them into a plain, galvanized iron bucket. They also look arresting in a wicker wastepaper basket, with a cleaned out gallon paint can hidden inside to hold the water, and other small wicker baskets make excellent holders for dried flowers.

In fact, I use all sorts of baskets for flowers and leaves – bread and fruit baskets, shopping baskets, little sweetmeat baskets, children's baskets, garden trugs and ornamental baskets, because straw, wicker and raffia, being natural substances themselves, blend successfully with all plants. Paintings by Chardin, the 18th century French painter, and early 19th century watercolours, often show flowers arranged in baskets.

Baking dishes of all kinds are always useful, from roasting pans to oblong

Browsing round a hardware store or kitchen department can yield a surprising number of unusual and useful containers for flowers, plants or bulbs.

perb for a
casion, par-
lowers and
nn. You can
y are sadly

y favourite
lovely little
ases, which
tumn roses
ived these.
round; in
ach spring
lets, prim-
forget-me-
fritillaria.
specimen
-fashioned
st months,
oneysuckle
mble from

ases were
ps. People
m because
y England
gle bloom
be used
f arrange-
rames can
a tiered
graph on
men vases
adding a
esk.
obtained,
nulate the
est-tubes
n use in

most of
nmended
modern
not de
They ar
they
rest
in
f

Whatever the style of the objects and furniture in a room, containers for arrangements can be very simple. In a sophisticated Park Avenue apartment, an ordinary galvanized bucket holds a splendid arrangement of dried grasses, corn, teasels, gypsophila, sunflower and other seed heads. It stands proudly on a fine 18th century gilded console table.

loaf tins, to round cake tins and shallow pie dishes. I use large shallow baking tins to float flower heads, such as tulips, hollyhocks, camellias and begonias, like lollipops and the effect is stunning. Cake and loaf tins may be used for mounds of flowers, such as hydrangeas, cut hyacinths, lilac, stock and sweet William.

Take a walk round your local iron-monger's shop and just look at the variety of shapes and sizes of reasonably priced kitchen utensils. If you stop filling them in your mind's eye with food and start imagining them full of flowers, a whole new area will suddenly open up.

Junk shops, jumble sales, country markets and auctions are natural places in which to rummage for interesting and bargain flower vessels. Here again, train your eye to see the unusual. An old-fashioned water carafe looks charming filled with mixed seasonal flowers on a bedside table. Those old stoneware kitchen jars which used to hold salt and flour, look just right holding country garden arrangements of such flowers as tiger lilies, eucalyptus leaves, lime flowers, gypsophila, choisya, daises and larkspur. They also set off autumn displays of berries and coloured leaves or dried flowers, or simply branches of glossy *Magnolia*

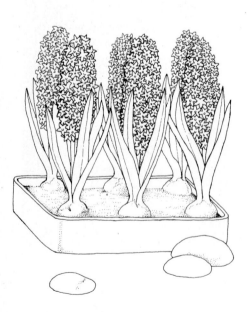

Hyacinths are best grown in large groups of one colour in shallow geometrically-shaped containers; a rectangular pottery serving dish is ideal.

grandiflora foliage. *Magnolia grandiflora* is a beautiful evergreen magnolia with large blooms. It originated in the southern areas of the United States, but is reasonably hardy in cooler climates if grown against a wall for protection.

Big, undecorated dairy jugs, churns, old cream bowls, sinks, galvanized hip baths and earthenware farm crocks are all attractive and useful for flowers; and I use an old pottery baking dish, picked up in a sale, to grow indoor hyacinths!

However, except for the larger jugs, I do think that flower containers should not have handles. So, avoid old teapots and cups and, worst of all, china and silver sauce boats.

The makers of medical and pharmaceutical glass receptacles provide an unexpected but unrivalled source of containers for flower arrangers. Beakers, vials and test tubes are manufactured in a multitude of shapes and sizes which cannot be bettered as flower vases and which are obtainable from hospital supply shops. I sometimes use a medical phial as a specimen vase to hold one rose, or a piece of Aaron's rod, or an onion seedhead. Placed to the right of the fireplace, with a picture to the left, it gives a fresh, stylish look.

In fact, any plain glass vessel is good. The glass may be clear, or bubble glass from Biot, amber, white, smoked, delicate green, pale or very dark blue. (Examples of these can be seen on many of the illustrations here, such as those on pages 11, 24 and 35.) But I do not think red, bright yellow, or bright blue are suitable, as these colours will kill rather than enhance the colours of the blooms.

There is only one kind of glass receptacle which I find totally unacceptable and it is, incidentally, the most expensive. The wildly elaborate, modern, cut-glass vase should be avoided on all occasions because it is vulgar and ugly and puts the kiss of death on the best of flower arrangements.

There are 18th century cut-glass flower vases which are enchanting and highly suitable for flowers, if you are lucky enough to own or find one; but this is because the workmanship then was delicate and gave the right feeling in ways the modern versions never do.

Another container from the past which I like is the *Epergne*, which the Victorians used so much. They are elaborate and take rather a lot of

flowers, but they are s
dinner party, or special o
ticularly when carrying
fruit intermingled in autu
still find them, but the
becoming more expensive

However, I know that
ideas from the past are the
18th century specimen v
you can see filled with au
on page 14. John Fowler re
I use mine all the year
spring, for examples of
flower in every vial – vi
roses, sprigs of blossom,
nots, lily-of-the-valley and
In summer, they hold
bloom from each of my ol
rose bushes and, in the cold
winter jasmine, cyclamen, h
and *Viburnum fragrans* tu
them.

Originally, specimen v
probably developed for tul
were enthusiastic about the
of their rarity in 18th centu
and they were displayed a si
at a time. These vases ca
separately, or for pairs o
ments, or the two wooden f
be placed together to forn
circle of vases. The photo
page 54 shows a set of speci
used for this original purpose
touch of colour to a library d

Charming replicas can be
or the flower arranger can si
same effect with a few glass
and a rack, such as childre
school chemistry laboratories

One of the advantages of
the flower holders I have recor
so far and, indeed, of nearly al
containers, is that they are
signed to narrow into a neck.
usually as wide at the top as
at the base and so there is n
tion to the number of flowers
arrangement through lack
for their stems.

Many traditional arrangeme
originally dictated by the desig
traditional flower vase, which
was a development of the class
This started out in histor
receptacle for carrying water
a narrow neck to prevent spill
to hold flowers, for which
patently unsuitable. Therefor
better not to buy vases, new
with narrow necks, if you
avoid hours of frustration.

Although I break most of n
rules every now and again, ther
I do not break in any circumances

Above: Medical or scientific glass phials make useful and unobtrusive vases, as well as being attractive objects in themselves. Here two Algerian irises (Iris stylosa), placed in a wide test tube, stand on a table in front of late 18th century coloured engravings.

Left: Tulips look best cut to the same length, keeping them in blocks of one colour. Here a regimented group of 'London' tulips are placed in a clear rectangular glass tank, so that the green stems and leaves become part of the colour build-up.

I always like to have two blooms at every season of the year on my desk in the country. Even at the bleakest moment of the winter, I will have a spray of, perhaps, winter jasmine or early buds, while throughout the summer I like to have roses.

I never tolerate plastic vases, flower containers or flowerpots. If you are going to grow flowers in pots, use earthenware pots.

My strong feelings on this subject stem from the simple fact that plastic flower containers are not yet properly designed. The majority are trying, impossibly, to be imitations of china, earthenware, or even basketry; the worst offenders being plastic *cache pots*, pierced white or brilliant green, with serrated rims. Plastic flowerpots should be beige, dark aubergine, deep, deep moss green and other original colours to match entirely original designs using this material, but no-one has come up with them yet. They have been very badly considered.

But, if you are landed with some monstrosity as a gift from a well-meaning friend or through a moment of blind folly, do not despair. Provided the shape is right, you can often do a lot to improve a container.

I once bought a jade cactus in New York. It arrived in a rusty rectangular petrol can. This was supposed to be put inside an expensive container, but I simply took some white rope, wound it round and round the can and secured it at the top with strong adhesive. It looked very handsome. Rope is very useful and will wrap and disguise almost any shape.

Paint is the great standby. You can have even very small tins made up in almost any colour you like, or you might try mixing your own; either way, the ugliest objects can frequently be transformed into acceptable containers by being painted white. Modern aerosol spray paints are useful for this purpose.

So, when buying, look at the shape first and remember that you can always change the colour later.

Once you have the right flowers, the right arrangement and the right vase, it is worth spending a little time considering them in relation to light. If they are placed on a table in front of the window, or on the windowsill itself, all the light comes in from behind and you will lose their colour during daytime.

I nearly always arrange flowers on a table, so that they are near or under a table lamp and are lit up by it in the evening. If you have a modern installation, it is worth training a spotlight on them. My spotlights have dimmer switches with which I can adjust the strength of light shining on the flowers, because a scorching light will make them wilt and will also kill delicate colours.

I do not think you can have too many vases. They do not really take up much room and it is worth building up a collection, which, as we have already seen, is more a matter of using initiative than any great expenditure. A good collection gives you the freedom to use different containers at different times of the year and in different places and so help to create the variety and interest to the eye that is so important.

Left: Dull containers, whether vases or pots, can be improved by winding thin rope or string around them. (Coat the surface with glue beforehand.)

Mixed late summer roses are shown to advantage in individual test tubes, in a wooden stand which was modelled on an 18th century design. They are lit by an electrified double candlestick.

Flowers and plants for city situations

Though flowers are less abundant in cities, they can be used to enhance urban interiors. In the Fifth Avenue apartment shown left, the Foujita in its white linen frame needs severe flower arrangements, such as the bronze and white chrysanthemums massed to the left and right of the brown silk velvet covered sofa. Orchids (above), would contribute to the formal colour build-up of a city living room like this.

Living in the city does not mean that you must buy all or even most of the flowers you require for your home. It is true that the town dweller rarely has access to a large garden, or to woods and hedgerows. However, this is not an insurmountable problem and, indeed, there is a certain advantage to being in this situation. It can make your whole involvement with flowers positively exciting, if you learn to approach it in an unconventional way.

Firstly, the person living in a town house or apartment should concentrate on growing, rather than on cut flowers. This does not imply a restriction of choice to the usual indoor plants – although these, too, have a useful and ornamental place in city apartments. I am referring to growing garden flowers, which may seem surprising and even impossible to those without gardens: but, in fact, it is incredibly easy and there is no reason why your home should not be filled to overflowing with flowers if you wish.

Not only garden owners can have

Right: The bead plant (Nertera granadensis) grows well in a pot producing a colourful mound of orange berries.
Below: Any town house can be brightened with a simple window box of geraniums, lobelia and alyssum, all of which are remarkably trouble-free, as long as the box is watered regularly.

pleasure from the seed catalogues produced by all the major seed suppliers. City dwellers should send for them, too, and spend as many happy hours browsing through them and deciding on next year's flowers. A simpler method, though less fun, is to go to your local garden shop or department store and buy packets of annual seeds and lots of earthenware flowerpots. Then you are ready to start.

Use all available window space, inside with pots on the ledges and outside with window boxes. Remember that, above all, in their natural habitat flowers need light and sometimes warmth, so try to simulate the growing conditions recommended on the seed packet. A warm window may replace the heated greenhouse and, instead of planting out, you can pot on into larger containers and simply open the window, or place the pots outside in the window boxes.

You may have some failures, of course, but most annuals are remarkably hardy. They want to grow and you will be delighted with the number of flowers which do appear.

While looking through catalogues, try to form a mental picture of how your selection of flowers will look in your home setting. The idea is not to grow just one pot of each species, nor even two or three. You should plant ten or fifteen. This will allow for some failures and still leave enough for a really spectacular display.

One of the most charming effects is created by plants which cover their containers entirely in a mass of tiny flowers. Rose-pink, lilac, white and purple alyssum, pale and deep mauve aubretia, compact lobelia (which is now available in white, scarlet and pink, as well as in the traditional variety of blues), and many small dense border and rockery plants, such as the crimson *Dianthus deltoides*, are all ideal for this. The bead plant (*Nertera granadensis*) may be used in the same way to form a ball of bright orange berries instead of flower heads.

The final flower shape is determined by the shape of the container. An ordinary flowerpot will produce a mound of flower heads, an oblong trough will produce a flower pillow and seeds planted in a round or oval container will grow into round or oval cushions.

Climbing and trailing flowers *en masse* also look very attractive. The easiest of these to grow are nasturtiums, which make a lovely, wild

waterfall of flowers. They need little care and actually produce more flowers in poor soil, so do not feed them. Ipomoea and convolvulus are also rampant growers, but do need the sun. Passion flowers do not mass, but look unusual and interesting, especially when trained to form hoops.

Black-eyed Susan (*Thunbergia alata*) is another delightful climber, which grows at astonishing speed and flowers over a long period. I like it best smothering a hanging basket. Columnea and *Campanula isophila* may also be treated in this way.

The only other type of hanging basket I find pleasing is one full of indoor ferns. This looks enchanting hung in a window or doorway with the sunlight filtering through the translucent green leaves from behind. But hanging baskets do require a lot of watering and, because they are often too heavy to lift down, you will have to climb to them daily and place a wide basin underneath to catch the overflow.

If you are a city dweller, or even if you live in the country, one of the most magnificent plants to grow in a pot is the sunflower. Plant the seed in fibre pots and, when the roots are beginning to show through these, put them into 20cm (8in) or 25cm (10in) pots and watch them rocket up. Give

them as much light and sun as possible, preferably placing them on a balcony until you are ready to bring them indoors. There is really no display like a corner of gigantic, ceiling-high, brilliant yellow sunflowers. Their height and scale can literally change a room from nothing into a sensation.

Hollyhocks are also delightful tall flowers, which may be grown indoors in the same way. There is a wide range of colours available, from white, cream and yellow, through all the pinks and reds, to an almost black purple.

A thicket of foxgloves (*Digitalis*) is another variation on this theme of tall flowers indoors. Their spikes of tubular flowers display intriguing markings of diverse colours, similar to the hollyhock range.

Everyone loves scented flowers and a number grow without problems inside. I dug up some of my scented-leaved pelargoniums this winter and took them indoors in pots, and they responded by giving a second flush of growth, just as they would have done in a warmer climate, such as the Canary Islands, where many of the flowers we are accustomed to seeing only once a year regularly bloom twice. The varieties of scented pelargoniums listed on page 63 are all suitable for the house.

Jasmine has the most exquisite

Above: Black-eyed Susan (Thunbergia alata) is a vigorous climber which I like best in a hanging basket.
Above right: Hot house nerines grow well in pots and have an interesting colour range of pinks, oranges and reds.

scent, and I am always torn trying to decide whether I love it even more than honeysuckle. Perhaps I would settle for honeysuckle in summer and jasmine in winter. Varieties of both can be grown in the town apartment.

The three jasmines I recommend all have white flowers and should be kept in control by pruning the stems before the flowering season. *Jasminum officinale* blooms in late summer; *J. sambac* in autumn and *J. gracillimum* in winter.

Honeysuckles are a little more difficult. The most successful are the two shade lovers, *Lonicera tellmanniana*, which has copper-yellow flowers, and *L. tragophylla*, with bright yellow flowers. Unfortunately, these two varieties are not scented. However, there is no reason why one side of a sunny balcony should not be covered with early or late Dutch common honeysuckle, so that the delicious scent wafts in through your windows.

Heliotropes grow well in pots. Cut them back to about 7cm (3in) at the end of the winter, then pinch out their tops when they are about 12cm (5in) tall, to make them bushy. Take cuttings in autumn to start new plants and your home will be filled with their heady scent.

A really pretty and unusual house plant, which I only recently discovered myself, is *Exacum affine*. For long periods throughout the year it is covered with little light blue flowers with yellow centres and it is scented, shade loving and very rewarding.

A pot of homely mignonette is child's play to grow and worthwhile, even though the flowers themselves are not showy, because it fills the room with the evocative fragrance of cottage summer gardens.

For those who like more formal blooms, the most scented of the gardenias is aptly named *G. jasminoides*. This grows to between two and six feet, with either double or single waxy white flowers, and needs plenty of light and sun.

Every plant lover has grown a bowl of indoor hyacinths and probably narcissus as well and I would not be without them in my home either. Their freshness and spring scents really do raise the spirits during the bleakest months of the year.

But do not ignore all other bulbs. One of the great advantages of town living is that your home is probably warmer and more sheltered than a country house. Central heating means that you can force early crocus, snowdrops, irises and freesias in your warm windows. Lilies-of-the-valley are a great joy and hippeastrum always appeal to me for their architectural qualities. These come in a variety of colours.

New bulbs should be planted in January in an average potting compost to half their depth in pots allowing not less than 2.5cm (1in) width of soil between bulb and pot wall. They need a warm temperature, 16°C (60°F), and no water for the first fortnight, then small amounts only. As the flower spikes appear, they should be kept well watered and fed with liquid fertilizer bi-weekly.

Lilies are the most wonderful flowers to grow indoors. They look and smell superb. They should be planted under 5cm (2in) of rich compost in a 15cm (6in) pot, watered carefully and kept at a temperature of 10°C (50°F). As they grow, they need regular feeding and plenty of fresh air, and they should not be disturbed.

To achieve perfect bowls full of bulb-grown flowers at the right time of the year, you do have to follow the rules. It is no good leaving them in the dark too long, or watering them too much, or too little and, as they grow, the bowls should be turned daily so that the plants do not lean towards the light.

Primroses, polyanthus, violas and grape hyacinths, nicotiana, stocks, sweet peas, African marigolds, pinks, petunias, the compact 66cm (15in) variety of Canterbury bells, blue lace flowers (*Didiscus caerulea*), asters – the variety Pinocchio has been specially developed for pots – the butterfly flower (*Schizanthus*) and even broom: these are just a few of the flowers many people do not associate with indoor growing. Yet they all provide good blocks of vibrant colour in a city apartment and I find them preferable to many of the more usual house flowers, which are often fussy and disappointing. The above plants are all happy growers and require remarkably little attention.

Experimenting with annuals in pots can be very absorbing for a flower-loving town dweller. There are continual pleasurable surprises and a great feeling of satisfaction as one species after another proves successful.

So many people work these days or lead very busy lives; therefore, sensitive and demanding plants often die of neglect. Because of this, I would avoid indoor azaleas, cyclamen and African violets. These have also become *clichés* among indoor flowers.

The age of plastic has also put me off several other plants, including begonias, whose big waxy flowers now look so artificial. I shall never really

Hanging baskets can be very attractive in porches, on balconies or in small conservatories. Ferns, such as Nephrolepsis exaltata (below left) are certainly best grown in this way, as are ivy-leaved pelargoniums (below).

like bird of paradise flowers (*Strelitzia*) again either, although I used to grow them and find them exotic, because almost indistinguishable plastic copies have spoilt them for me.

If you want to take trouble and spend time on indoor cultivation, you could grow gloxinias, which have splendidly showy, trumpet-shaped flowers. I love their velvet petals, jewel colours and rich green leaves. They need warmth and moisture and it is best to have several pots of one colour for maximum effect.

It would also be worth making an effort to prune and shape fuchsias the way the Victorians used to do. The end result of a tall cone absolutely covered with the dancing flowers is very striking.

Another inspiring and enchanting flower is the orchid. Do not imagine that growing these most luxurious of flowers requires forty years' experience, an expensively heated greenhouse and attention twenty-four hours a day. Many orchids are quite easy to grow indoors. Most of their needs are simple: a light, draught-free, sheltered position, a year-round temperature of about 16°C (60°F) and a rather humid atmosphere during their growing period. This is created by resting their pots on a tray containing a 5cm (2in) layer of gravel or pebbles with a 2.5cm (1in) depth of water poured into it, so that the base of the pot is not in contact with the water, but the air around the plant is kept moist through evaporation. *Maxillaria picta*, a creamy-yellow spotted with brown, lady's slipper (*Cypripedium insigne*), with brown, yellow and green speckled flowers, *Coelogyne cristata*, a white with yellow bloom and the small scarlet Mexican orchid, *Epidendrum vitellinum*, are all good indoor varieties.

Because there is rarely a garden in view outside the windows, those who live in cities should make more imaginative use of all their rooms for flowers and plants.

Herbs are a natural choice for pots in the kitchen window, or in a window box outside. Thyme, rosemary, mint, parsley, chives, summer savory, sweet marjoram, clove-scented bush basil and chervil are satisfying in numerous ways. They all smell good and improve one's cooking. They are ornamental and make the kitchen look fresh and, if you grow large enough plants, sprigs can be cut off to include in cut flower arrangements, too.

Moisture loving plants will be at home in the warm bathroom. *Philodendron scandens* and *P. erubescens* are two large climbing plants that do well there. So does maidenhair fern – a little forest of six matching pots is the most stylish way to grow this. Caladium, too, likes moisture and warmth and I like best the silver and pale green arrow-shaped leaves of *C. humboldtii*. Cyperus is semi-aquatic and one of the few plants which should actually have its pot standing in water. *C. papyrus*, the Egyptian paper reed of ancient times, grows 2.50-3m (8-10ft) tall and is much more interesting than the common umbrella plant (*Cyperus alternifolius*).

Far right: Culinary herbs can easily be grown in a window box, and look attractive as well as being useful. Right: Many people are nervous of growing orchids, though they are not as temperamental as you may think. They generally need a humid atmosphere which can be created by resting the pots on a bed of gravel, which is always kept wet.

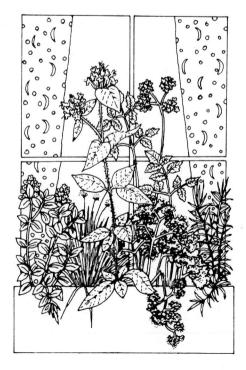

I would generally advise breaking away from the more commonplace plants, although I do have a soft spot for some old favourites, such as Busy Lizzie (*Impatiens*), so long as there are several pots together.

However, most of us must be bored with the sight of Swiss cheese plants (*Monstera deliciosa*) and the inevitable rubber plant (*Ficus elastica decora*) doing badly in almost every dry cleaner's window. They are over-familiar. Although I have seen really beautifully grown, immense, round bushes of rubber plants in the tropics, you would need a hothouse as big as one in Kew Gardens to achieve the same in a temperate climate! *Ficus lyrata* is a much more enjoyable variety, which can grow to about 3.50m (12ft) and has big, glossy, wavy leaves. I also like the staghorn fern (*Platycerium bifurcatum*) and *Schefflera actinophylla* has beautiful oval leaves divided into five leaflets, which eventually grow to 30cm (1ft) across.

Bonsai, the growing of mature trees to a height of between only 30cm (1ft) and 60cm (2ft), is too complicated an art to be dealt with in full here, but I do find these very fascinating indeed and particularly suitable for a modern or very disciplined city interior, a mature Bonsai is always acceptable. They

are the only miniature form of plant life that I like, but I do enjoy the idea of taking an immense oak tree and putting it on the dining room table.

The Indians and Chinese are reputed to have grown dwarf trees by the 9th century AD, but the Japanese took up the idea in the 10th century and developed it to its present form.

Bonsai are kept small in containers which restrict their root growth, and by pruning. A wide number of species can be successfully cultivated in this way, both evergreen and deciduous, and flowering and fruit trees are particularly enchanting.

You can grow them yourself, if you have a lot of patience and a long life; a slow-growing tree may take fifty to one hundred years to reach maturity. Or you may buy a young Bonsai and take it on from there. The major points to look for when buying are that the plant is small and attractive, with small leaves, and that the trunk is thick in proportion to the height.

Some lucky people actually find the occasional mature specimen growing wild on a rocky cliff or hillside, where Nature has done the work already, so it is worth keeping your eyes open.

If you are feeling rich, or you want to give a very special and almost everlasting gift, a mature Bonsai is ideal.

Above left: Many Mediterranean homes have a large pot of basil growing close to the kitchen both for its pungent scent and its delicious flavour. Though it is not a hardy plant, a pot of basil will thrive in any warm kitchen.
Above: Gloxinias are showy plants which enjoy warmth and moisture.

One is always lovely and a group of three or five, making up a 'table-scape', is strikingly dramatic. The Japanese never have a group of four, because the word 'four' in that language is similar to their word for death.

If Bonsai are beyond your patience and pocket, an indoor bay tree is always delightful and many people also like indoor orange trees, such as the small *Citrus bergamia*, with sweet, white flowers, or the Panama orange, *C. mitris*.

The hardy annual, burning bush (*Kochia trichophylla*), is a very satisfying plant in a pot, because it grows so rapidly to form a perfect 60 to 100cm (2 to 3ft) high bush; the fine pale green foliage changing to a coppery crimson in the autumn. Start it in heat in early spring and put it out on the balcony in late spring.

All the above plants, other than Bonsai, require a certain amount of heat, but, if your home does not have central heating, *Fatsia japonica* makes a good, big plant and you can also grow large bowls of hosta plants. They like moisture and shade and there are innumerable varieties, all highly decorative and very useful for cut flower arrangements as well. Baby's tears (*Helxine*) is a small, pretty plant which does well in cold, but frost-proof atmospheres and so does saxifraga and the climber, *Cissus antarctica* (syn. *Vitis antarctica*).

However, the one which appeals to me most is the aspidistra, that dear, old Victorian favourite, which is now rapidly coming back into fashion. Again, this plant must be kept in really good condition, as must all indoor plants.

Do make a point of caring for them properly. This does not mean they require a lot of work – they certainly do not need to be killed by kindness, as happens so often – they need regular and sensible treatment. Find out how much or how little water each likes; try to make it rainwater kept inside in the watering can overnight to reach room temperature. Feed them regularly; pot them on when they require it, because there is nothing worse than those stunted apologies which have been alternately drowned and parched, according to their owners' spasmodic memories, and are potbound in their original pot, so that their leaves are small, warped and desperate-looking, instead of being big, beautiful and glossy.

Left: The delicate green leaves of baby's tears (Helxine soleirii) could be grown in quite a cold place, such as a studio or garden room.
Below: A Bonsai of cypress is grown in a stoneware bowl with two rocks and moss to give the impression of a natural rugged landscape.

The square uplighter beneath this low, glass-topped table gives super translucence to the jade objects, each on its own perspex base, and picks out the fronds of the fern in its weathered terracotta flowerpot. The glazed pottery monkey is a late 19th century piece; the carpet is one of my own geometric designs.

Above: Children enjoy growing the pebble cactus (Lithops) which is one of the best mimics in the plant world.

Below: Climbing plants such as grape ivy (Rhoicissus rhomboidea) or the sweetheart plant (Philodendron scandens) can be coaxed into formal geometric shapes by training them round frames made from wire or cane.

Dirty leaves will never look glossy and dust is a great enemy of the house plant because it blocks up the pores, so that the leaves cannot breathe properly and it screens out the daylight that they need to live. Dust mature foliage first with a soft cloth and then sponge or syringe the whole plant with clean water. To heighten the sheen, wipe a proprietary leaf polish gently on to the upper face of each leaf with cotton wool. The resulting gloss will last for many weeks.

Although I like certain trailing flowers massed in a hanging basket, I find most foliage trailing plants straggly and untidy and I have my own special way of controlling them.

I train small-leaved species, such as ivy, tradescantia and *Zebrina pendula*, into geometric shapes with cane and wire netting. Four canes, each forming a corner in the pot and bound together at the top, make the basis of an obelisk, which is then filled in by training the plant round them. In the same way, I make cubes, squares, pyramids, hoops and balls of foliage. This is one instance when I do not expect or wish the plants to look natural.

My other method with such species is to train them into an artificial tree shape. All the stems are first trained straight up a single cane and then out over wire netting to form a ball of leafy branches, so that the end result is rather like a miniature indoor bay, which looks very well.

Bigger climbers like *Rhoicissus rhomboidea* and the devil's ivy (*Scindapsus aureus*) may also be trained into huge, impressive balls of foliage over chicken wire.

One of the tragedies of being a city child is missing out on contact with growing things, both animals and plants. However, although people in high-rise flats, or densely-populated areas are usually unable to keep family pets, other than cage birds, there are many ways in which the children's interest in living plants may be roused.

Children need to see quick results and vegetable tops provide a fast-growing source of fascination. As you prepare fresh carrots, swedes, radishes, turnips, parsnips or beetroots for meals, cut a half inch slice off the tops of two or three and give them to the child to stand in a saucer with just enough water to cover the bottom and place on the window sill. Shoots will appear within days and within a fortnight there will be full-sized leaves, provided someone remembers to keep them watered!

Pineapple tops will grow in the same way for a while, but it is better to put these into 15cm (6in) pots of sand to give them a chance to root.

Sprouting onions may be planted like any other bulb and will grow to about 45cm (18in) tall, producing a big ball of mauve flowers. The seedhead is ornamental and may later be used in dried flower arrangements. And who does not remember growing mustard and cress on damp blotting paper? Peas and beans will sprout and perhaps even produce flowers in much the same way, in a jar lined with damp, absorbent paper.

Children also love growing plants from fruit pips and stones. The climate of the country of the fruit's origin is the clue to the conditions it requires. Citrus pips will obviously need warmth; apple, pear and plum pips and stones are best grown in the cold. Like most seeds, pips and stones should be started off in the dark. Some stones, such as those of peaches, apricots and nectarines, should be cracked very slightly first and then planted in compost.

On the other hand, avocado, mango and lychee stones should be planted as they are and started off in warm darkness. It will be two or three months before they begin to grow and they should be kept out of strong light until their shoots are at least three inches tall. Although all these are slow growers, once they appear, they are very exciting; the lychee may grow up to 2m (6ft) in a year.

These plants not only give children an idea of the sources and development of life, but they provide delightful foliage plants for adults too.

Other plants I would suggest, as much for the way they intrigue adults as for children, are the sensitive plant *Mimosa pudica*, which folds up its foliage when touched, and the insectivorous plants, sundew (*Drosera*) and Venus' flytrap (*Dionaea*), which are always good for a thrill or two of horror. The former traps and digests insects in the sticky red hairs which cover its leaves and the latter has leaf lobes which snap closed to imprison and digest any insect foolish enough to land on them.

A more pleasant idea is a little bowl of pebble cacti (*Lithops*), which always enthral children and make a pretty addition to any side table. I use them in the same way as I use my bowls of sandalwood shavings, *pot pourri*, lavender and sunflower seeds, for textural interest.

The only other cacti I like are really large varieties that may be used as single architectural features.

Although so many flowers and plants can be grown indoors, living in town does mean buying more flowers than country people do, not only for the home, but especially to take to friends.

To me the most rewarding florists' flowers are lilies. They are bought by the spray and, while you often have to

Avocado stones are just one of the many pips, stones and seeds from ordinary household produce which can be grown into attractive plants. Start them in the dark, then bring into the light when a shoot appears.

This small town garden has been turned into the equivalent of a cottage garden with charming results. Space is used very cleverly: hanging baskets, tall fuchsias grown as standards, climbing geraniums and other wall shrubs cover the walls and dividing trellis, while plants grown in pots and tubs keeps the existing beds free for the tall-growing plants.

pay per bloom, there are usually only one or two out, all the others following later, and they are superbly romantic. Orchids are for special occasions as they are very expensive, but they do last and one looks good in a single vase under a spotlight. Carnations are always a good buy, especially in winter; so are the very big, white, in-turned chrysanthemums. Freesias, with their haunting perfume, are always welcome.

I would categorically avoid commercially grown roses, because they have no scent, no shape, no glamour and are very difficult to keep. The African violet is another plant on which people spend a lot of money to give as presents. However they are dull because they nearly always look seedy and sickly once removed from the professional hothouse.

On the other hand, our own garden violets are delicious and I use them to

break one of my own rules – that highly coloured containers should not be used for flowers – putting them in a little bright blue glass vase on a table covered with blue *objets d'art*.

If cut flowers are bought as a gift and need to be transported any distance, recut and try to condition them at home for an hour or two first. Then put them in a plastic bag with damp paper or moss round the base of their stems. They may also be transported in sealed plastic bags in which they will remain fresh for a long time.

The great thing about buying flowers for friends is not to mind if the recipient has the sense to cut the stalks down. Commercially grown flowers always have immensely long stems which are a disaster to any arrangement, unless it is a very big, romantic one. Carnations, especially, should not be left on long stems in a fog of asparagus fern. They look best cut

short and made into neat pincushion arrangements.

Flowers for a city home have to be very differently conceived from flowers for an entrance hall in a country house, or a sitting room in a cottage. In London, I find the most satisfactory arrangements are flowers of the same variety bunched firmly together, or perhaps one stem of a lily in a specimen vase. Trying to give romantic country treatment to florists' flowers is very difficult because the extra foliage and wild plants which are necessary are simply not available.

If you are fortunate enough to have even a tiny garden, or just a balcony in town, here are one or two basic hints on how to use it to the full, although it is not possible to go into the subject of the small garden in any extensive detail here.

It is most important to plan the use of every inch of the limited space available, so that none is wasted. This means looking at the garden or balcony, vertically as well as horizontally. Fences, walls and railings provide the extra dimension, so aim to cover them all with an abundance of rambling, trailing and climbing plants.

Wisteria, honeysuckle, clematis, climbing roses, hydrangeas and solanums will give you flowers for your arrangements as well as vertical richness, and trained pyracantha and cotoneaster may be cut for their berries. The annuals, nasturtiums and Canary creepers, will cover a wall or balcony rail in a season and so will the fast growing annual hop, *Humulus japonicus*.

If, like many people, you only have a narrow yard behind your town house, build a small pergola over part of it and train a vine, or Virginia creeper to turn it into a shady cave to block out the sight of the surrounding houses.

In such a very small space, do not attempt to grow grass, as there will be too much wear for it to look anything but scruffy. Turn the yard into a patio by laying paving stones, or, if you must have turf, plant chamomile or creeping thyme. Paving may be set like stepping stones across this, but both herbs are tough enough to stand up to a certain amount of use and they also smell interesting when pressed underfoot.

As with indoors, use massed pots of flowers to create a feeling of lush growth in both patios and balconies. I saw this done to great effect in Mr

Nehru's garden in Delhi, where there were literally hundreds of flowerpots containing every kind of English annual.

I would say that some of the most beautiful gardens I know are the smallest and they are owned by people with far less money than some of my clients, who own acres of hideous herbaceous borders. Town gardens can be immaculate, with every plant watched, tended and fertilized and tiny, perfect gardens can be made out of the smallest basement area.

However limited the space, do keep a corner of it for at least one shrub. Try to choose a shrub which will give the most value over the longest period of time. For example, *Choisya ternata* is an evergreen which will keep the garden looking fresh and alive in winter. It has pretty, scented flowers, as well scented leaves and its attractive foliage

A 'green' garden is stylish and trouble-free, and ideal for a small, shady town garden or back yard.

Foliage, shrubs and evergreen plants can be made into spectacular arrangements. Above are some of the most attractive. Left to right: Choisya ternata (Mexican orange blossom); Daphne laureola, the spurge laurel; and Ruta graveolens (rue).

may be cut to back up your commercially bought flowers and give them a more individual look.

Evergreen daphnes are also useful in this way and the rue, 'Jackman's Blue' (*Ruta graveolens*) is an intriguing small, grey-blue, aromatic shrub with intricate, lacy foliage. The best escallonia is 'Iveyi', with large, dark, glossy, evergreen leaves and masses of dense panicles of white bloom in late summer. Everyone should also grow a patch of hostas for their sculptural beauty as a growing group and for individual leaves in flower arrangements.

Given an average town garden, I do not think you have to choose between using it for cut flowers and using it as a handsome place to look at and enjoy. Assuming that you do wish to be able to gather flowers there, it is better to have several of one plant, than one each of many; several rose bushes of the same type and colour, rather than a number of different varieties. Then you may pick for the house and still leave plenty of blooms to make a good garden display. If you go about the planning and the actual planting with care, there should be sufficient flowers to fulfil both needs.

Many people who love old-fashioned roses, as I do, are often unaware that there are a number of these which are particularly suitable for the small garden. They grow to approximately 1.30m x 1m (4ft x 3ft) shrubs. Among these are the shell-pink Victorian scented rose, Baroness Rothschild; the lemon-tinged white alba rose, Félicité Parmentier; the damask, Comte de Chambord, with rich, lilac-pink flowers and an intense scent; the small 60cm x 60cm (2ft x 2ft) china rose, Cramoisie Superieure, which flowers throughout the summer in crimson clusters; the small moss rose, Little Gem, with crimson blooms and great fragrance, and the clear pink musk rose, Empress Josephine, which is known to have been cultivated for at least two hundred years. All make unusual and inspiring additions to a town garden. Rambling roses can also be grown, and are especially effective for screening the garden.

From this, I hope it will be seen that flower lovers who live in the city, may still indulge extensively in their hobby. A certain amount of thought, some forward planning and a lot of imagination will often result in more stylish flower ideas and original displays than those we are all accustomed to seeing in the country.

This delightful town garden shows the potential of even the smallest area. A pergola has been built against a dividing wall and climbing roses have been allowed to cover it completely. Here there is plenty of scope for cutting both flowers and foliage, while at the same time, flowering plants and small shrubs soften the rather angular dimensions of a newly-built garden.

53

Flowers for mood and occasion

Flowers contribute to the mood and feeling of different rooms. On the early 18th century writing desk (left) which already held a 19th century clock and three dried allium flower heads, I placed a specimen vase holder with a number of different tulips. It gives an exciting richness to an already crowded desk top, adding to the typical country house atmosphere. On the other hand, in a small London flat I relish a casual bunch of flowers (above) to enliven my simple objects when I entertain.

One interesting way to use flowers is to create or enhance a mood. Even primitive tribes arrange and strew flowers and foliage to mark the highlights of their lives, and we are not so different. The coming of spring, the gathering in of the harvest, and the principal religious festivals are all traditionally celebrated with flowers in every society, and it has been so since before history.

Who does not carry the memory of certain flowers which marked a special time for them? Ever afterwards, the sight of those blooms is enough to bring back that precise memory, however long ago.

A bowl of hyacinths in a room immediately takes me back to the Februaries of my youth, with the fires burning and snow falling; and the smell of wallflowers reminds me of summers then, because my mother used to grow them under the dining room windows, so that the scent would waft into the room. Each autumn, the fruits and berries and coloured leaves remind me of that first joyous autumn arrangement I made when I was an adolescent.

Our classic festivals are, perhaps, the only times when I am happy to let tradition take over. At weddings, there is nothing prettier than those grand, romantic flower arrangements decorating the church and matching the formality and nature of this great celebration; fresh sprays of blossom, daffodils and mimosa for spring, opulent masses of cabbage roses and peonies and lilies in summer and luxurious confections of huge, white chrysanthemums and foliage in autumn.

For the bride, the traditional florist's idea of a bouquet of white or pale sorbet-coloured, scented flowers is perfect. However, an adventurous bride does not really have to relate her bouquet to her wedding dress. If she is wearing yellow, she may carry a pink and white posy. A blue dress could take yellow flowers and a pink dress could have a blue nosegay, and *vice versa*; although I really prefer the old-fashioned style.

At the wedding reception, again I like the full-blooded Victorian centrepiece of carnations with garlands of asparagus fern looped at the edge of the tablecloth; but this is the only time I would ever use this combination. Asparagus fern has no place in home arrangements.

Christmas is also a time when traditional ideas are best. I like a Christmas tree that is either highly conventional with multi-coloured balls and tinsel, or one which is very stylish with tiny, white, electric candles and only silver decorations.

The German idea of having real lighted candles and no other decoration on the tree is also charming, but, should you decide to do this, you must obtain the specially made holders for them. Place and light the candles with extreme care, and only when the tree is new and still damp. Once the needles begin to fall, it is no longer safe to have an open flame near them.

The idea of a plastic Christmas tree is repulsive and I cannot imagine anyone who likes plants and flowers ever contemplating such a thing.

Perhaps my dislike of plastic imitations is the reason why I do not care for poinsettias. There are so many artificial versions of this plant around and it does not have, itself, that fresh, living look which is the basis of the attraction flowers have. However if enough are massed together I rather like the pink variety.

As fresh flowers are scarce and expensive at Christmas time, this and other winter festivals such as Thanksgiving are best catered for by marvellous dried arrangements, which are brought out for the winter months and put away for spring and summer in plastic bags. In this way, they do not gather dust and are not left round the house to become over-familiar.

You may prefer to keep just one special dried flower arrangement to be used only at Christmas, and an attractive centrepiece for the table is to have a vase on to which you can build a pyramid of evergreens and coloured balls.

My chapter on autumn and winter gives the fresh flowers and foliage available from the garden at Christmas. Because they are so few, they are best displayed in single or specimen vases, or as small posies.

Easter, on the other hand, is the most exciting period for flowers, with all the spring bulbs at their best. To me, this festival is more symbolic as a time for renewal than New Year. Winter has gone, the trees are in bud and the gardens carpeted with early daffodils and crocuses. It is the most invigorating time of the year, a time of promise, when the air tingles and we feel again that we can tackle anything and everything, successfully.

Often the family gathers, or friends come to stay. There are picnics and

Above: A traditional Christmas tree with real candles is one of the most attractive decorations for this time of the year.
Below: A charming idea for a table centrepiece is to surround a candle with dried flowers.

A rather conventional but charming
mixture of small flowers: blue gentians,
pink dianthus, daisies, and other white
and silver flowers and foliage evoke the
mood of a Victorian 'fête champêtre'.

outings and it is fun to hold an Easter supper party, too.

Cover one or more simple, circular tables each with a different shade of yellow tablecloth to the ground and give each a different arrangement of either bulbs in bowls, or cut spring flowers: crocuses, daffodils, forsythia, freesias and primroses, to make a symphony of yellows, Easter's colour.

You could do a variation of this in orange, rust and scarlet for Harvest Festival, or in mixed reds for a family Guy Fawkes night.

There are so many intriguing things one can do with flowers when friends come for a meal. A container, little larger than a thimble, holding a single ipomoea, or an apple blossom, or a rosebud, two primulas, or a sweetly perfumed philadelphus flower may be placed at each setting. Sometimes I do slightly larger, mixed, individual arrangements in those little, old-fashioned bedside water carafes. If you cannot obtain these, plain modern carafes would be just as good.

Herbs are very neglected assets to a dining table. Many of them are strongly scented, and their scent always enhances the smell of good food. Use bunches of parsley, my old favourite watercress and another favourite, chamomile, which I love for its pungent smell and tiny, star-like flowers. This is pretty bunched on its own or in three pots round the table, or included in the individual posies. Sages, thymes and mints are all decorative in a dining room.

You should ring the changes when you have guests. It is not always necessary to have one ornate centre-piece. Sometimes, you may prefer four arrangements with perhaps a china object in the middle and, at other times, a pair of arrangements equidistant from each other gives a pleasing balance. The only really guiding rule is that the flowers do not interfere with people seeing or talking to each other across the table.

The temptation to use objects as intrinsic parts of flower arrangements has to be treated very carefully.

Once objects are introduced, the arrangement is in great danger of becoming 'arty-crafty'. There is a very fine dividing line between what is good and right and stylish, and something which just misses all this. Two fritillaries in a very small glass container on a chimneypiece with the right objects around them can be all right, but a stiffly arranged mini-

bouquet is all wrong, because it is too contrived. Flowers nestling in satin, or velvet, sprigs of coloured leaves arranged round a violin brooch to denote 'music', miniature and bottle gardens are, to me, as lacking in taste as plastic garden gnomes.

I realize that this is a very personal view, but I am a very definite person and my views on good and bad taste are, of course, inextricably tied up with my approach to every aspect of design. Designers and clients in America, France, Italy, Australia, England and even Japan, have turned the style into a movement. I originated part of it, and was influenced by other parts, and others have been influenced by me. It is a feeling, the look of today, just as every period before has had its own special style.

Those earlier styles are rewarding to explore through flower arrangements, because, like music, flowers can be evocative.

In decoration, it is interesting to see the way certain colours have been fashionable in certain periods. In the early eighteenth century, heavy dark colours were popular, rich olive greens, glowing reds, sombre browns and beiges together with searing Chinese yellows. Later in the century, translucent pastel colours were used – pinks, blues, greens and a great deal of white. The Regency period revived the rich and dramatic colours again, but used them with brilliant lemon yellows, turquoise blues and bright, raspberry pinks.

Personally, I revel in the drab khakis, deep maroons and the dark chestnuts and indigo blues often incorporated into heavily patterned Victorian wallpapers and fabrics and reflected in their huge, evergreen houseplants.

The Edwardians preferred lighter colours – pale honey, slate grey, pinks and creams; and the 'twenties pro-duced some very violent colour shocks: sickly jade greens, vivid purples and repulsive rusty oranges.

In the 'thirties came the off-white interior and colour did not really return in a big way until after the Second World War, as a reaction to the austerity of those years.

Throughout all periods, flowers were always displayed in ways which blended with the decoration and you will find this reflected in old paintings, carvings, decorated porcelain, silver and engravings. From these sources the favourite flowers of the times and

Below: An unusual idea for an Easter lunch party is to cover circular tables with floor-length yellow cloths, and have a different arrangement of yellow spring flowers on each.

A nosegay of herbs at each place
setting is a charming idea for a dinner
table. They can be made up with fresh
or dried herbs, but should be as sweet-
smelling as possible. I like to make
highly individual nosegays, trying
to suit each to the personality of
every guest. I use herbs such as sage,
rosemary, mint, lavender, artemisia,
lemon balm, scented geranium leaves,
and centurea, surrounding one or more
scented rose-buds, and with the
addition of tiny flowers such as
forget-me-nots, saxifraga, lobelia
or alyssum.

the ways in which they were arranged can be seen, and you can use them for inspiration.

So many of the flowers we know now did not exist in Medieval times. There were no daffodils, tulips, lilacs or pinks, but a 15th century painting shows a single white lily in a pewter jug, and Raphael painted lilies and roses with fir branches on a Roman ceiling.

It is especially worthwhile looking at the flower paintings by the 17th century Dutch masters, such as Van Huysum, who specialized in the first large pictures of mixed flowers in rich and varied colours, with roses, tulips, peonies and lilies together with fruit and vegetables.

Although I do not make this type of arrangement myself, and I am not normally in favour of slavish copying, in this case it is an absorbing idea to try to bring these paintings back to life in your own flower arrangements. Alternatively, they can be used as starting off points for your own interpretations. However, you will need an abundance of blooms for this particular style and so it is perhaps restricted to those with brimming gardens, or to the very special occasion for city dwellers who have to use shop-bought blooms.

By all means do giant sunflowers like Van Gogh and old-fashioned roses like Fantin Latour. There is, in fact, a Centifolia rose, with cupped pale pink blooms and a delicious fragrance, called 'Fantin Latour' after this painter.

Even on Regency porcelain you will find pretty floral paintings and there are glorious heaps of flowers and fruit heavily carved on the choir stalls of some of our cathedrals. All are sources of information and inspiration for flower arrangements.

Victorian style is probably the easiest to reproduce, because it is very clearly defined. The Victorians were particularly fond of conservatories and heated greenhouses, which inevitably meant that there were a great number of pot plants brought in and taken out of the house at different times, partly to give variety, but also to rest the plants from unsuitable household conditions. Most homes had the inevitable aspidistra, along with the china fireplace pekinese.

They liked very formal, tidy, circular arrangements and a lot of ferns in *Epergnes*, and the Victorian posy is familiar to everyone, a charming, neat cushion of flowers to be carried in a young girl's hand or placed on a dressing table.

Their desire for order made them masters at training plants into geometric shapes, both in the garden and in the house, where everlasting helichrysum and dried flowers were made into balls, or flower trees, or heart-shaped cushions, and even fuchsias were painstakingly pruned into tall cone and pyramid shapes, hung with graceful flowers.

Mauve was the colour much favoured from the Edwardian era to the early twenties. For instance, when Lady Willingdon was Vicereine of India, she had such a passion for mauve as a colour that all the flowers in the immense Viceregal garden were a variation on mauve.

The garden, filled with such flowers as violet tulips, crocuses, violets and lilac in spring, followed by purple anemones, asters, delphiniums and clematis, and mauve buddleia, daphne, hydrangeas and roses in summer, was the triumph of the great architect and designer, Sir Edwin Lutyens.

This idea can be brought most effectively into an indoor arrangement. There is also nothing more reminiscent of pre-war public occasions, nights at the opera, or days at the races, than huge bunches of white mop-head hydrangeas spectacularly crammed together.

An arrangement which was only seen in the late 'twenties, and can be used to remind us of then, was a big Lalique vase full of arum lilies. You never see this now, as people do not usually use arum lilies on their own, but generally mixed with other flowers.

Of course, it is not necessary to take a period or a painting as your theme. You may take a country such as France, Italy or Spain, and do an arrangement of some of the flowers you saw there on holiday. Hibiscus flowers will transport you to the Bahamas, where they appear on lunch tables every day.

You may take a country theme – harvest perhaps – and fill a wicker wastepaper basket tightly with ripe, golden corn. Or you can use a mood – pink roses in a simple, white, pottery cylinder for romance.

Try old French roses and peonies under a gilt Georgian-style looking glass on a marble chimneypiece for nostalgia, and strangely coloured chrysanthemums in a glass vase next to a weirdly shaped piece of rock; search for *cousinage* or contrast.

Above: A white form of hibiscus with a prominent red staminal column. An arrangement of hibiscus could lend a Caribbean mood to a lunch or dinner table.

Below: Some people may like to use things seen in museums, such as this intricately designed Persian carpet, as a starting point for arrangements.

Many ideas may be found in old books, in hidden corners of antique shops, churches, or on cracked pieces of china, as well as in museums and art galleries. In a host of unexpected places the ghosts of bygone flowers in carvings, paintings and porcelain are waiting to be brought to life again.

It is not only the sight of certain flowers which brings back memories, or creates specific auras. The scent of plants. and flowers matters almost as much to me as their colours and construction. It is one of the most vital ingredients in the atmosphere of the house.

I exploit this sense in all sorts of ways and not only through flowers. For instance, I personally love the smell of a coal fire and, if you are lucky enough to have open fires, you could do as we do at Christmas and burn a different type of fire in each room; coal, wood and peat for their different smoky aromas as much as for their brilliance and warmth.

The smell of genuine wax polish on wood, instead of those sickly scented aerosol sprays, is another household smell I enjoy and, just before winter dinner parties at/ home, we have our own version of burning joss-sticks. This is to carry a smouldering stick of dead, debarked juniper through the drawing room and dining room. The scent, unlike that of joss-sticks or burning perfume, is not strong enough to kill the fragrance of the flowers, but still hangs deliciously in the air.

Scented flowers can play powerfully on the emotions. Crushed leaves of choisya seem cheering and lemon verbena has what might be described as a happy scent. The first scented narcissus raises the spirits to a peak of hopefulness and the old herbalists claimed that the smell of certain herbs was a powerful aphrodisiac!

There is the faintest air of sadness about the smell of pine and nothing could be more nostalgic than the scent of that exquisite transparent, shell-pink alba rose, 'Celestial', whose fragrance has been known to flower lovers since the tenth century.

Even the word heliotrope makes me remember the place and the day and the hour when I first smelt its warm sweetness over twenty years ago. The rarer white variety is even more strongly scented than the popular purple cherry pie, and a pot of them brought indoors on a summer's day will fill the whole house with fragrance and also last much longer than cut blooms.

Scents also evoke the seasons. The freshest, lightest scents come in spring with narcissi, new leaves, particularly the Balsam poplar, and violets, joined by apple blossom, freesias and the stronger scent of hyacinths. Lily of the valley and the common, scented azalea follow and then comes the heady explosion of summer: roses, lilies, sweet peas, wallflowers, pinks, mignonette, nicotiana, phlox and stocks. Autumn has its special earthy smell typified by the chrysanthemums and heathers to match the falling leaves and rain and the fungal smell of the woods. The strong, sweet perfume of *Jasmine nudiflorum* and rich conifers mark winter.

Many shrubs are rewarding sources of different scents spreading through the year. Purple and white *Daphne mezereum* blooms in February and March, along with its sister, the ever-green *Daphne odora*, which has intensely fragrant purple flowers. There are two rhododendrons with scented foliage, *R. rubiginosum* and *R. salvenense*.

The Mexican orange blossom, *Choisya ternata*, blooms in May along with lilac and three more Daphnes, *D. x burkwoodii* (syn. *D.* 'Somerset'), *D. cneorum* and *D. blagayana*. *Skimmia japonica's* white flowers appear in June, with philadelphus, the mock orange, flowering in June and July, then buddleia attracts clouds of butter-flies to the garden with its honey scent.

Even winter is surprisingly rich in scented flowering shrubs, the most deservedly popular being jasmine and

Hydrangeas are particularly useful for interesting arrangements on a large scale. This is Hydrangea macrophylla mariesii, a delicate pink hydrangea with a flat flower head. All hydrangeas are extremely decorative; some cut and dry well, while others are best grown in pots.

Right: An arrangement of pastel pink and white scented flowers, redolent of the style of English country houses between the wars.

Below: Stephanotis has a fabulous scent though it needs warmth. I like it trained round circular or other geometrically shaped wire frames in the Victorian manner.

the winter-flowering honeysuckles. The evergreen sarcococca is not very impressive to look at, but it has the most delicious smell and flowers in January and February. *Viburnum fragrans* flowers from November through to spring, at the same time as *Mahonia bealii's* perfumed yellow racemes are in blossom.

Foliage must not be overlooked in the search for fragrance. At home I grow many pelargoniums especially for their scented leaves. The peppermint-scented *Pelargonium tomentosum*, and rose-scented 'Attar of Roses', and three lemon-scented varieties, *P. crispum*, *P. citriodorum* and 'Mabel Grey' are among the most popular, but nutmeg-scented *P. fragrans* and balsam-scented *P. filicifolium* are also pleasant. These pelargoniums are not only available all the year round, because they are easily grown indoors, but they all have attractively shaped leaves, which add to the architecture of any arrangement.

Choisya has scented leaves and flowers and the lovely, blue-grey leaves of eucalyptus have a special smell when you press them with your fingers. The curry plant, *Helichrysum angustifolium*, really does live up to its name and, among the silver leafed plants, *Artemisia abrotanum* and *A. absinthium* are also strongly scented.

Many people are completely unaware of the enormous range of herbal scents, the mint family being one of the most extensive and including Eau de Cologne mint, apple mint, pineapple mint and, of course, peppermint, as well as catmint and many other varieties.

Thyme, too, has a number of variations, the most popular being *Thymus citriodorus*, which is lemon-scented as the name suggests. All the sages have well defined scents, so do chamomile and marjoram, balsam and rosemary and the aniseed-scented fennel, but one of the nicest of all the scented herbs is lavender.

Small vases or nosegays of herbs placed on tables in the house create a most haunting blending of essences and I sometimes hide one or two stems in a flower arrangement.

If you want to know whether you would like the scents of some of the plants I have mentioned, you could visit a garden for the blind, where the flower beds are all raised and only scented flowers are grown. The parks department of your local authority will probably know where you may find the nearest of these gardens. It is wise on such a visit to keep in mind that flowers change scent according to the weather and the time of day, some giving more scent in hot sunshine and others after rain, some in the evening and some at midday. And one plant changes scent quite drastically after picking – the elderflower, which fills the hedgerows with such overpowering sweetness in spring, smells objectionable after a few hours in the house! (Perhaps its greatest value is as the chief ingredient of Constance Spry's Elderberry Sorbet.)

It is worth considering every aspect when arranging flowers for atmosphere, or to celebrate an occasion. Their colours, their shapes, their scents, their interaction with each other and with the objects around them and with their position; where they are placed in relation to where people sit and stand, and even their textures all combine in the final effect. The ways in which they can be used and the moods and auras they can evoke are almost infinite. Use your imagination, forget the conventional *clichés*, and experiment.

Flowers
for all seasons

There is no need to be without flowers or plants in the house at any time of the year. The great pleasure of spring and summer is the abundance of full blooms and strong colour, while the great pleasure of the winter months is the severity of the cool, neutral colours. I am never afraid of mixing patterns and using violent colour contrast (left), while the crisp texture of dried arrangements (above) can work splendidly with objects of subdued colour.

Spring

In cool northern countries, spring flowers are welcome signs of warmer days to come. It is especially nice to see masses of them brightening street corners on flower-sellers' stalls.

Spring is the renaissance of the plant world. Everything is beginning to shoot up and, to me, it means delicious, fragrant flowers. Scent is a vital ingredient of most of my arrangements at this time.

The first to appear is the snowdrop and I dig up the bulbs and put them in a shallow bowl just before flowering. I also pick really big handfuls of fifty or sixty of these flowers to fill short, wide containers. Those people who believe that snowdrops have no scent have simply not gathered them in sufficient quantity. *En masse*, they have the freshest and lightest essence, which perfectly symbolizes early spring.

Crocuses also have great charm when dug up and brought indoors to flower in containers and they are lovely

as forced pot plants. However, if you prefer them cut, they should be picked as pencil-thin buds and brought into the house where they will burgeon forth within an hour. I gather them just after breakfast, when they are just white tubes and, by lunchtime, they are great big, showy, beautifully open blooms. But you may have to pick them again next day, as they fail quickly in the warmth, unless still growing from the bulb.

Do not mix the colours. Have white, purple or yellow and, again, plenty of flowers. If you do have several varieties, then have several vases, with only one colour in each.

Primroses, violets and lilies of the valley are all flowers which I dig up and bring in, and which I also grow in pots, because they last longer this

way. When the flowers die, the plants can be returned unharmed to the garden, if they have been handled with care.

A good spring idea is to have three vases of the same shape and size on a table and fill one with primroses, one with yellow narcissi and one with yellow daffodils, a build up of yellow colours which gives great effect. Generally, violets should be treated in the same way as primroses, all cut to the same level to make a cushion. It does not matter how small the container is, it can be 5cm (2in) square, but they must be packed together. I find that one of the best receptacles is a round, white *soufflé* dish.

It is usually effective to crowd a whole lot of flowers on short stems into squat containers, so that the flower heads are seen as a mass. Sometimes, this method of grouping may sound repetitive, but, just as Ikebana is the only Japanese way to arrange flowers, this is my recipe: although I think I make more exceptions than the Japanese do!

For example, I would not treat camellias like this. These should look in the vase much as they look growing on the bush. They can be arranged in single colours, all white, all red or all pink, or they can be mixed. They need a rather good, solid container and may branch out to a certain extent, because this is a very romantic shrub and, to my mind, infinitely preferable to the rhododendron.

Perhaps I do not care for rhododendrons because of an association of ideas dating from the time spent at a preparatory school I disliked in Surrey, which is rhododendron country. A few individual blooms are attractive, but paradoxically they often seem artificial growing on the bush. The camellia has much more useful foliage, which is shiny and looks brand new all the year round.

However, there are two rhododendrons with mammoth leaves which I think are highly acceptable. *R. sinogrande* has dark, shiny leaves 80cm (30in) long by 30cm (12in) wide and *R. macabeanum* has 30cm (12in) long leaves, dark green with an off-white under-surface.

Generally, my inclination is to isolate the bloom of this shrub totally from its foliage, which is pure idiosyncrasy. But there are two exceptional varieties and both are scented. *R. ciliatum* is a dome-shaped bush with bell-shaped rose-lilac flowers and the Chinese *R. auriculatum* grows into a small tree with rich trusses of white flowers in July and August.

I do not often use the common yellow azalea indoors, but its delicious scent in a warm corner of the spring garden is a must. I never use hawthorn, because it is unlucky in the house and does not last, but I would not be without its heady aroma nearby and its bright haws in autumn.

Spring posies are always a joy to arrange. I do not necessarily see these as being comprised only of small flowers. A posy is essentially a bunch of flowers, the stalks of which are all cut to create a very slightly dome-like, spherical shape and, in this season, nothing is fresher than mingling all the early blooms and flowering shrubs. Posies may have quite a lot of leaves to fill them out or may be just solid flowers.

For small posies, a mixture of violets, or primroses with forget-me-nots, or small daffodils with crocuses, is delightful. Grape hyacinths (*Muscari*) and *Gentiana verna*, the small, pure blue, April flowering gentian, make an arresting combination. Anemones need to be used on their own, either in multi-colours, or all reds together and all blues together. They do not last long and have no scent, but they are cheerful little flowers.

A spring bouquet could be a bunch of fairly concentrated blooms, some of which must be scented, and freesias, narcissi, primroses and tulips are a good combination.

Freesias alone are wonderful, especially for their evocative scent, but also for the delicacy of their colours and form; although, if you have only half a dozen, they need to go in with other flowers, otherwise they look spindly in a sparse, vague arrangement. I prefer them actually growing in wide pots, but the alternative is to keep them low, compact and massed on short stalks.

Daffodils epitomize spring for most people and they are usually so inexpensive that bunches can be bought to supplement those grown in the garden and form a big drift of dazzling yellow indoors. It is much more effective to put four containers full of narcissi and daffodils together to make one huge display, than to spread them about in small amounts, or you can have a huge low basket massed with blooms.

For me, the arrival of tulips is a great event. What could be more exciting than a wide vase of black parrot tulips, all cut to the same length and crowded tightly, so that they become an irridescent, ragged mass. Mixed tulips are also very pleasing and, on the whole, they should be cut with rather short stems and heaped together, otherwise they tend to flop all over the place (even after careful conditioning). Another way to display them is to place one bloom in each opening of a replica Delft specimen vase, which I would paint white, because I think the blue and white of the copies is fairly unsympathetic to tulips compared to the 18th century ones.

The other flower which comes instantly to mind at the thought of spring is the hyacinth; its rich scent takes us back to childhood Sunday

The two flowers which mean that spring is really on its way, are primroses (centre) and snowdrops (below). I like to dig up clumps from the garden and bring them into the house in pots, so that they can be replaced when flowering has finished.

afternoons spent round open fires. The Victorians used to grow them in strange glass vases by a method known as 'hydroponics', which is the growing of plants without soil. The bulb is held in the specially shaped top of the vase, with its base just above the level of the water in the ballooning glass below. It should be started in the dark, then turned daily after being brought into the light, so that it does not grow in one direction only and finally fall over. Modern versions of the vases are available from many florists.

Oddly enough, an ideal container for growing hyacinths is a $30 \times 20 \times 10$cm ($12 \times 8 \times 4$in) pottery tray. The bulbs should be planted regularly in rows of three so that twelve of them come up as a solid clump of blooms all the same colour. Bowls should always contain one colour only, but several bowls or trays may be grouped together to make up chromatic blocks.

The other pot flowers which look extremely attractive in massed matching groups at this time of the year are primulas, but they also look well cut and used in vases. Hippeastrum should be force-grown singly for their architectural value, they have fine heads of trumpet-shaped flowers and are available in super white, pink, vermilion and rich deep scarlet colours. The pots should then be put outside to 'rest' in the garden from June to September.

There are one or two later arrivals which I tend to avoid cutting. Wisteria fades very quickly and looks much better left romping over a wall than in a vase. I also find lilac tricky; the leaves are dull and so I strip them all off on the rare occasions when I pick this flower, split the stalks and concentrate all white blossoms together, all purple together and all mauve together, so that they look really luxurious.

I have never found laburnum usable. In fact, the only way I have ever seen it even grown successfully was by Lord Astor at Cliveden as 5m (15ft) high trees in big pots inside the house.

Early spring is the time when city dwellers make their first weekend excursions to the countryside after winter and when country people go out to cut horse chestnut and balsam poplar branches for the sticky buds. Later, I take a single white chestnut flower and put it in a vase on its own. It does not last long, but it is very effective.

Pussy willows appear on *Salix caprea*, long golden tassels hang from *Salix medemii* and bright yellow catkins

decorate the hazel. All should give the flower arranger a great deal of pleasure when gathered and displayed in generous sprays. It is best to be bold and carry in an armful, so that, once they are in the container, there is the interest of hundreds of twigs intertwined and criss-crossing each other.

I do pick wild flowers, too, but carefully, leaving the rare and threatened species firmly alone. Many are in danger of becoming extinct and are soon to be protected by law, so leave the wild orchids and cowslips for everyone to enjoy and stick to celandines, which are ravishing related to primroses and crocuses in three small vases.

Bluebells I associate with hanging out of bicycle baskets, dying as they near the metropolis. They are also extremely difficult to arrange and I really think they should be left where they grow, as a carpet under the trees.

Bridging the gap between spring and summer, narcissi, daisies, carnations, white rosebuds and a dried herb make a charming centre piece in the dining room of a country house in Holland which I decorated.

Summer

Lilies, roses, hydrangea heads and hollyhock spikes are concentrated casually in a corner, bringing the richness of summer into an 18th century dining room.

Summer is so generous with its flowers that they really need an entire book to themselves. They climb and ramble and tumble and explode from every available patch of earth and in every corner of the garden there is so much waiting for the flower arranger.

Old-fashioned roses are a passion of mine and the flower I like most in the world is the sharp pink bourbon 'Zéphirine Drouhin'. I have several on walls in my garden and it seems to me to be one of the most perfect of roses, with its intoxicating scent and its length of blooming period.

The classical forms of old-fashioned roses, from the purity of the dog rose (*Rosa canina*) to the luxurious opulence of the cabbage rose (*Centifolia*), to the blowsy, heady damask rose, are what real roses are all about: rich, exuberant, superbly balanced and fragrant. In comparison, I find many modern roses dull, flat, lacking both in quality and scent.

The old roses are the roses of poets and ballads down the ages: the queen of flowers. The Cretan palace of Knossos has a mural of a rose known to have been painted 3,500 years ago. Six hundred years before the birth of Christ, they grew in the Hanging Gardens of Babylon. Greek and Roman statues were adorned with them and the people wore rose crowns at their festivals.

To hold an old rose in your hand is to step back in history. 'Celestial', the shell-pink alba rose, has grown unchanged in form since the late 10th century, and *Rosa damascena versicolor*, with its deep pink and white flowers, is the rose traditionally believed to be the rose of both York and Lancaster. The bourbon, 'La Reine Victoria', takes us back to the paintings of Fantin Latour, and a huge bush of the common moss rose may be the direct

descendant of one planted in the same spot a long, hot, Edwardian summer ago.

People tend to think of old-fashioned roses as taking up an enormous amount of space, but I have already mentioned some which are suitable for the small garden (see page 52) and there are others which grow no more than 1m × 1m (3ft × 3ft). Most of the larger varieties do not require careful pruning; if necessary they can be cut with shears to keep them within bounds, once they are mature.

The other misconception about these roses is that they only bloom for a short season. This is true of some: alba, damask, centifolia, moss and gallica roses usually flower only once, although there are exceptions and, in the case of the gallicas, this flush is spread over at least six weeks. However, bourbon, china and musk roses will bloom throughout the summer, or flower in two long flushes, and many varieties also have attractive hips for autumn arrangements.

They all look superb in flower arrangements, either on their own, or with peonies, or in romantic mixtures of summer flowers, such as lilies, pinks, poppies and *Alchemilla mollis*.

It may offend purists but I use old-fashioned roses with modern ones. This is partly because of the contrast of the constructions of the blooms, but much more in order to be able to use the widest possible variety of colours. Old roses only have blue-pinks and reds in their colour range, while the modern hybrid tea roses also have orange-pinks and reds, and I love the exciting vibrancy of these colours together: the modern apricot H.T. 'Whiskey Mac' with the magenta pink 'Bourbon Queen', or the vermilion 'Super Star' next to the cerise pink Gallica, 'Belle de Crecy'. I suspect that this is the very reason why other people do not put the two types of roses together. Perhaps they are afraid of the dramatic impact of colour.

My own garden is designed basically as a cutting garden, with roses as the principal flowers. Although I gather as many flowers from it as I need for the house throughout the year, it is also a pleasant garden in its own right because of the shrubs and climbers grown there; the walls and hedges; and the pool and fountain, so that it does not matter how much I cut, the garden is still attractive.

My favourite modern rose is 'Peace', which starts blooming in mid-June and goes on until the end of November – and sometimes into December. About twenty bushes of this variety are grown in formal beds in the middle of the garden, especially for cutting. Yet, they are always decorative with buds coming on or extra blooms which are not required in the house. My old-fashioned roses grow in the side beds. A 'new' old-fashioned rose I particularly like is 'Constance Spry'.

Geraniums and pelargoniums of all colours and shapes are grown too, but in pots and tubs.

I suppose one of the highlights of these months which I look forward to each year is the first honeysuckle bloom. With its wonderful scent, this lyrical, utterly simple flower touches many mixed arrangements with magic. My favourite variety is *Lonicera periclymenum belgica*. It also has a special fascination for me because the

Rosa gallica versicolor is another beautiful old-fashioned rose, otherwise known as Rosa Mundi. It is often confused with Rosa damascena versicolor, the rose of York and Lancaster, but it is almost certainly a sport of Rosa gallica officinalis.

honeysuckle motif is used extensively in the earliest architecture and recurs again and again on furniture, columns and buildings.

I am also attracted to acanthus by the same architectural connection. This is the leaf of the Corinthian capital. *A. mollis* is the most popular but, in my opinion, the more attractive is the smaller *A. spinosus*. Ivy and globe artichokes, too, have an architectural quality in the structure of their leaves and their extraordinary heads. Cardoons (*Cynara cardunculus*) are related to these and have the advantage of being hardier, as well as inedible, so I use the leaves for fresh arrangements and dry the heads for winter. The decorative thistle (*Echinops*) is in the same category.

Foxgloves (*Digitalis*) are very handsome flowers when cut on long stems and used, half-a-dozen together, all standing absolutely upright, and, in this context, we should not ignore the onion family (*Allium*). There are so many types, ranging from the big, starry, dried seedheads down to the little yellow flowers of spring.

I like many herbaceous plants, but not in borders. I prefer them intermingled with other flowers and vegetables as in a cottage garden.

My romantic summer vases are dependent on lilies, for their fabulous scent, and on peonies to blend with the roses; and Canterbury bells, nicotiana, irises, bergamot and lychnis are used extensively.

The sight of phlox immediately takes me back to the apple orchard at the house in Essex in which I was born, where the phlox grew every year in the same corner. Use one type massed in a vase, or mingle with other seasonal flowers, but do not put different varieties and colours of this flower in the same arrangement.

Marigolds I love, because they are prolific and easy and among the few really brilliant orange flowers we have. The English calendula is much hardier than the African and French marigolds and makes a splendid splash in a long, low, oblong or square container on a low table.

One of the charming customs in Paris in midsummer is the way all the small florists have little mixed cottage posies for sale. This is something English florists rarely do and it is a pity, but, if you have a garden, you may make them up for yourself.

Cornflowers are useful for these are very agreeable when massed together in low arrangements. Candytuft is also a good addition to summer bunches. Love-in-the-mist is pleasing when growing, haunting when softening a miscellaneous vase, and ravishing dried. Sweet peas and pinks both have the charming old world prettiness one looks for in a country posy; pinks like rose-buds, also look exquisite with the silver leaves of *Senecio cineraria*. Sweet peas have the advantage that the more you pick, the more they grow and I like to see them cut short and grouped by colour, all pale pink, deep, deep amethyst, and white, all placed in the same vase.

Pansies, zinnias, and sweet Williams can all be used in the composite summer posy and I even cut delphiniums short and include them for their beautiful range of blues. I find them rather unsympathetic to arrange alone, without other blooms.

A little flower which looks very effective concentrated in small bunches is the petunia, especially the vivid, star-striped varieties.

As most of my flower arrangements are supported and balanced by foliage, a large number of shrubs grow with my old-fashioned roses in the side beds of the garden. Bushes with scented flowers, such as choisya, Daphne, philadelphus and the little myrtle, as well as camellia, London pride (*Saxifraga umbrosa*), with its dark green whirls of leaves and feathery, pink flowers, the calico bush (*Kalmia latifolia*), evergreen hypericum and *Ceanothus burkwoodii*, with its masses of bright blue flowers, are invaluable used in mixed summer bunches, or on their own.

People so often neglect to look at and use the old shrubs in the corners of their gardens. Perhaps these have been there so long that no-one really notices any more, or perhaps they were already in the garden when the new owners moved in, part of the landscape, but unappreciated. A friend of mine had a garden full of magnolia, choisya and philadelphus and had never cut any of them for indoors, until she saw one of my foliage arrangements. So, do use the branches of any old, familiar shrubs to fill out your arrangements during all the seasons of the year and, if you are planning to plant shrubs and only have limited space, remember that evergreens are the most useful to the flower arranger.

Most magnificent of all is *Magnolia grandiflora*, the evergreen, which is usually grown as a wall shrub. Its big, shiny leaves last a long time and I grow it specially for use indoors. Although the large, creamy white flowers are difficult to arrange, and they only last about a day and a half, the scent is overwhelming. It is easiest to take just one bloom and put it with a single leaf in a specimen vase, although four or five with lots of foliage in a larger container look very good, too.

There are many who dislike hydrangeas, but I like the mophead and lace cap varieties, as well as climbing hydrangeas, whether they are growing outdoors, arranged in water or dried. White hydrangeas are superb and very evocative of the gracious Edwardian era. Even the vulgar, striking pink is enjoyable and useful. This plant fills the gap after the flood of summer flowers is over and before the autumn

blooms appear and, of course, at the end of its own flowering season it fades into a remarkably beautiful range of rusty pinks, greens and pale mauves, all of which dry to even subtler colours.

Buddleia is grown to attract butterflies into the garden and, indoors, it is used in the larger, romantic summer arrangements. I also cut the blooms with 12cm (5in) stems, remove the leaves, and crowd them, like so many lollipops, into a square container.

Among the leaves I grow, use and admire in the garden are, of course, hostas, which I have mentioned briefly before, but which are truly indispensible. They make excellent ground cover, with the added advantage of growing bigger leaves when planted in the shade. *H. crispula* and *H. albom arginata* are green with white borders; *H. glauca* has huge, grey-green leaves; and is the best. *H. fortunei robusta* has deeply veined, heart-shaped, bluish leaves and *H. ventricosa* has very large heart-shaped, deep green leaves. There are also many other varieties.

One of the most striking foliage plants is *Arum italicam marmoratum*, which is large and marbled, as is its cousin, *Arum pictum*. Some sages also have attractive foliage, which smells interesting, too, including *Salvia officinalis tricolour*, with bluish purple leaves splashed with cream and magenta.

For grey and silver foliage, I turn to my eucalyptus trees, for the delicate discs which give an almost ethereal texture to fragile arrangements. The silky, fernlike *Artemisia pedemontana* and *Centaurea gymnocarpa* have different qualities of lightness and, in this colour range *Senecio laxiffolius* and a number of the santolinas have pleasing leaves.

Summer is a wonderful time for wild flowers and I treat them in a very luxurious way by having lots of one species together. Do not overlook weeds. White nettles are very attractive, and another of my favourites is the pungent chamomile, with its daisy-like flower, and many grasses have a freshness when green, and can be left in the vase without water to dry automatically for winter.

Old man's beard (wild clematis) and hops both give a trailing, winding softness to country arrangements. The lime-green flowers of wild parsnips, lady's mantle (*Alchemilla*) and a number of the spurges, especially sun spurge, are unusual additions to all-

Plants have inspired architects and designers for centuries. The Greek Corinthian capital was based on the acanthus leaf; while the national emblem of Scotland was based on an ordinary field thistle.

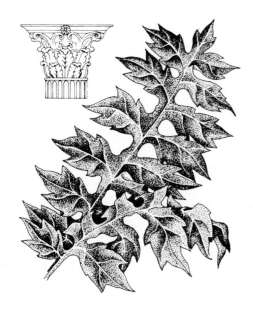

green arrangements, which I love.

Sweet cicely (*Myrrhis odorata*) is an aromatic, splendidly sculptural plant, and giant hogweed, which grows up to 3m (10ft) tall, is magnificent, but must not be confused with hemlock, a 2m (6ft) tall plant with similar white flowers, but poisonous ferny foliage in place of hogweed's harmless ovate, segmented leaves. In this architectural category, I also like big bunches of marsh thistles, which grow to between 1m (3ft) and 1.75m (5ft), or one specimen of a 1.75m (5ft) tall Scottish thistle, with its stiff, silvery spines.

This is really the time of year when even the flower arranger may go wild. There is nothing you cannot do. The gardens, hedges, woods, roadside verges, fields and commons are brimming over with flowers to satisfy every whim and please the most critical eye.

Show romantic medleys of flowers, or neat, heaped cushions of flower-heads, or single blooms in specimen vases, or formal arrangements, twin bouquets, related containers, chaste posies, or unsophisticated bunches.

Vibrant pinks are brought together in this luxurious cushion arrangement of different old-fashioned roses, placed on a marble-topped table between Chinese cocks and pink quartz elephants.

Autumn and Winter

Gourds are ripe for picking in the autumn and are among the many decorative possibilities for the colder months of the year. I prefer them massed in a bowl or basket, as above: just two or three gourds in a bowl are pointless and uninteresting as an arrangement.

Autumn is a marvellous time for scavenging. Every corner and hedge has drying plants, interesting seedheads and curling, tinted leaves. The most important object of the autumn arrangement is that it should express the fruitfulness of the season and, because these are the most bountiful months, you do not have to be rich or grand to be able to do this with great luxury and style.

In a large, wide container you can mix berries and fruit with flowers and foliage. Many of the ingredients I use can be gathered from the roadside, saved from the compost heap, or discovered among the despised weeds in the garden.

Berries should be massed. Do not ignore trailing branches of blackberries with the contrast of ripe and unripe fruit together. I also use trusses of tomatoes. There are one or two ornamental species which produce plum and pear-shaped fruits in reds and yellows – 'Tigerella' bears red and gold striped tomatoes, and 'Tangella' has brilliant, tangerine coloured fruits. As these are also delicious to eat, you have the best of all worlds.

Sloes, hips and maize cobs can be heaped with sprays of yellow, red and purple berried barberry and scarlet-berried cotoneaster.

The excitement of autumn is in creating extraordinary combinations, like *Iris foetidissima* seedheads, with their bright orange seeds, and red

Vitis coignetiae leaves; or aubergines, green and red peppers with clusters of cob nuts and grey and red cabbage leaves; or even beetroot leaves, which look great with red dahlias.

When Terence Conran, who created Habitat, came to lunch with me last October, I knew he had very understated tastes and there was no point in buying a lot of expensive blooms in London. So I took a large circular vase and made a complete autumn bouquet of the last of everything in the year; roses, rusted a little by the first frost, old man's beard, dock leaves, just turning red, and their Venetian-red seedheads, a spray of crab apples, a sprig of *Rosa moyesii*, with its striking scarlet hips; it was a great, wild ball of

In a beige panelled breakfast room this arrangement of hostas, fennel, hellebores, artichokes, blackberries and figs gives a wonderfully cool, fresh look on an early autumn day.

autumn rubbish, which most gardeners would just have thrown away – and it looked very well.

Specimen vases do come into their own now, as there are so many snippets of plants and solitary, late flowers which look good in the group of slim, individual containers: the very last wisteria blossom next to the first of the chrysanthemums, orange berries on a mountain ash twig, next to a sulphureum lily, a meadow saffron (*Colchicum*) and some red oak leaves.

Most people are unaware that many spectacular lilies are at their best in September, including the Turk's cap varieties, *Lilium henryi* with orange blooms, which grows to between 2m (6ft) and 2.25m (7ft) tall; *L. speciosum* with white, crimson spotted blooms; and the orange tiger lily, which grows up to 2m (6ft). I like to have one flower in splendid isolation in a vase.

To warm up the house on a cold, late September day, use vibrant reds, pinks and mauves. A glowing display might be made with mauve and crimson elder foliage, dried dock seedheads, the last of the season's claret red and scarlet roses, two or three sprays of the old, shocking pink, climbing rose, 'Zéphirine Drouhin', and some bergenia leaves just turning colour.

The bergenias are an unbeatable foliage family for the flower arranger, the largest being 'Ballawley Hybrid', the leaves of which may be 25cm (10in) across, bright, glossy green in spring and turning to crimson in autumn. Other varieties go purple, orange and mahogany at this time of year, the most colourful being *B. delavai* and *B. purpurascens*.

As the flowers become thin on the ground late in this season, I sometimes do arrangements of all leaves and just one or two blooms. Six blood red sedums, choisya and one pink rose would make a good medium-sized composition, with the sedums grouped on one side and the rose off centre.

The leaves I do not care for in September and October are the inevitable beech and copper beech. The beech is one of the noblest and most beautiful trees, but it has no place in flower arrangements, because it has become a hackneyed autumn statement and looks boring. The same applies to copper beech, which reminds me of third rate boarding houses.

Other trees which have foliage which turns to rich and vivid colours are oak, prunus, Japanese maple and mountain ash, all of which turn red.

The most dazzling of the acers, *A. palmatum septemlobum* goes on incandescent red and *A. japonicum* becomes a riot of orange, yellow and scarlet. The rhus turns scarlet and orange and tulip trees, poplars, birches and hornbeams all go yellow. Cut big branches of them.

Another subject for this treatment is heather, where the question of scale and the right container is very important. I saw off great hunks of it to stand in buckets and it looks very handsome on the floor, the level at which nature makes it grow.

Among the little flowers I like best at this time of the year are meadow saffron, or autumn crocus (*Colchicum*), which are delightful picked for small vases, or dug up and brought indoors in pots. They fascinate me particularly with their remarkable ability to produce flowers without water or earth. If you place the bulbs on a saucer in the window, the flowers will bloom without any more attention; although, after flowering, the bulb should be planted in the garden if it is to bloom next year.

I use very few dahlias, but the red ones may be included in mixed arrangements and I find an immense, sulphur yellow bloom very effective standing alone in a cylindrical vase.

Bamboos also make excellent architectural features in a room. Cut them long, about 1m (3ft), and use them massed. There are various types; some have brilliant green leaves striped with silver, others gold striped leaves and *Phyklostachys nigra* has an interesting shiny, deep purple stem. Bamboos are evergreens, but, as they do not originate from a temperate climate, they should only be cut in the middle of summer and early autumn to allow them time to recover from the previous winter's frosts.

Asters are cheerful flowers in October for their mauves and pinks in mixed vases, or to brighten a room on their own. Their colours are well set off by a shiny, black cylinder vase.

The deep yellow and rich brown of rudbeckia make it appealing, although I do not mix it with others, but cut it short and crowd it into squat containers to make pillows of flowers.

Bowls of gourds are an attractive seasonal-idea, but they must be arranged in generous proportion to give them guts. I have seen too many bowls with just three or four gourds in them and this does not work. You must have lots to achieve the correct scale. When they dry and become a mottled cream colour, I think they are particularly intriguing – but that is when most people throw them away!

An unusual idea in the autumn is to dig up a clump of fungi – toadstools from the woods or mushrooms and puffballs from the fields and put it in a rectangular container. There is an amazing number of species, many of which grow in naturally balanced groups and look fascinating on a dining room table. I also occasionally pick one really big fungus, about 25cm (10in) in diameter, and place it alone in a basket. This can be very effective.

While it is true that there are many fewer flowers in winter, there are still more than is generally realized. People with gardens forget to plan for this season, which is a pity because most of the shrubs which bloom in the coldest months flower for far longer than the summer shrubs.

Viburnum fragrans is covered with pink buds and white flowers and *V. bodnantense* 'Denen' has thick clusters of white flowers from November to spring at the same time as many of the summer flowering viburnums carry bright red fruits. The long lemon-yellow racemes of *Mahonia japonica* hang heavily from late autumn until early spring and the variety 'Charity' has large sprays of deep yellow flowers during autumn and early winter.

'Winter sweet' (*Chimonanthus*), lives up to its name by producing pale green or yellow flowers, with rust or purple stained centres on leafless branches at this time. The purple flowers of *Daphne mezereum* are ready for the New Year, and all the varieties of the Asiatic shrub, corylopsis, produce exquisite tassels or racemes of flowers, in late winter. Sarcococca is sometimes known as Christmas box, which quite accurately describes it.

The special pleasure with all these plants is that their flowers are scented, and they are joined by the two winter honeysuckles, *Lonicera fragrantissima* and *L. purpusii*, which flower from January to March and are absolutely lovely to have in great trails in the house, because they are so unexpected.

Garrya elliptica is the best known of the evergreen garryas, with long grey-green catkins in January and February; and another plant I enjoy is the witch hazel (*Hamamelis mollis*), with its large, fragrant, golden-yellow flowers from December to March.

I do not normally mix winter shrubs which are in flower, but prefer

to bunch them in individual vases, although, of course, I do use evergreen foliage with bought, or late blooms.

The chaenomeles start flowering in late January and continue until the end of May in a wide variety of colours – white, salmon pink, orange, scarlet and crimson. They provide a marvellous splash of colour very early in the year and branches in large containers have a strong oriental appeal.

The winter flowering cherry (*Prunus subhirtella autumnalis*) is the best of all, so delicately covered with semi-double, white flowers from November to March and there is a bush variety too. Do not just admire the blossoms on the trees. Cut great branches and bring them in. The petals drop all over the carpet, but it looks very pretty.

A number of other prunus also flower in winter, but not over such a long period. The Chinese peach (*Prunus davidiana*) carries white, or rose coloured blossoms on leafless branches between January and March; the Manchurian apricot (*Prunus mandshurica*) is rarer, with peach pink flowers in February and *Prunus kanseunsis* has pink-tinged white blossom in February.

Throughout the winter I pick crab apple branches for their long lasting scarlet or orange fruits which cluster on the branches from autumn until the blossoms come the following spring. In mid-winter I cut Scots pine and use it on its own. If you cut a well-shaped branch, it is rather like having a Bonsai on the table. I prefer conifers alone, rather than mixing the colours, although the blues and silvers make interesting combinations: for instance, light blue-grey *Chamaecyparis fletcheri* with the darker *C. allumii*, or the silvery blue cedar (*Cedrus atlantica glauca*) with the Kashmir cypress (*Cupressus cashmeriana*).

Dogwood, too, makes excellent architectural displays with its extraordinary red and yellow barks. Branches of box are surprisingly practicable, as they are always very green, shiny and fresh and last for several weeks. And, among the other foliage I gather, are choisya, eucalyptus, evergreen magnolia and even its poor cousin, laurel.

Most households have at least one or two indispensable bowls of hyacinths during the cold months and I also have pots of scented jasmine. I bring in sweet geraniums, bergenia, hostas and even *Verbascum broussa*, for its downy white leaves. Quite by

chance, I discovered that all these can be happy indoors, so you must experiment. Try everything once and you will soon find out which plants are contented to winter inside, and which are not.

There are also quite a number of small flowers which carry on bravely through the winter. The wonderful Algerian iris, *Iris stylosa*, is undoubtedly my favourite. The first blooms appear in the middle of November and it continues flowering until the end of March. It is the most rewarding of winter flowers. Pick them as thin, pencil-like buds and, within half an hour of being placed in warm water, they are in full bloom. One alone, or four, or twenty or a mass of sixty – in any quantity they are really exciting. As plants, they grow well in poor soil, but take time to establish in the garden and need a warm position. We grow ours in front of the house, where they are protected by walls.

Winter cyclamen (*C. orbiculatum*) flowers in pink, crimson or white from January to April. It has a pleasant scent, naturalizes easily in the garden and, in my opinion, is infinitely preferable to the tender hothouse varieties.

Helleborus is another large winter flowering family. The Christmas rose (*H. niger*) has its white flowers from December to February, the green hellebore (*H. foetidus*) produces jade green flowers in January, and, in February, the large lime-green flowers of *Helleborus corsicus* appear in clusters too. They look wonderful indoors.

The yellow, buttercup-like flowers of winter aconite (*Eranthis*) are rather small to cut, but they are so charming that it is definitely worth while digging up a patch of tubers in mid-winter and bringing them indoors in pots. They can be returned afterwards in the same way as snowdrops and crocuses.

If you do not grow many of these shrubs and flowers, it is a good idea to use your specimen vases, as I do, to catch and display single late blooms which appear, because some winters can be quite amazing. One year, I remember the marigolds bloomed right through and the choisya bushes were covered in flowers in November. If you do not prune your roses until spring, they quite frequently have a number of blooms at Christmas, and here and there in the most sheltered crannies of the garden, there are often surprises hiding. Put together, all these make interesting and unusual mixtures of flowers for the winter months.

Opposite: Although they make a mess, large extravagant bunches of winter berries give tremendous life to a room in winter, as seen here towering over the Cloisonné bears on their glass cube bases under a Chinese porcelain lamp. Below: Flowers that brighten winter months before bulbs begin to bloom. Centre: the Christmas rose (Helleborus niger); below: the winter aconite (Aranthis hyemalis).

The use of everlasting flowers

I find that almost all flowers and leaves dry in an interesting way. This 17th century Nevers vase has more and more leaves, seed heads and flowers added to it each year – box, banana, allium, Vitis coignetiae, hydrangea, bracken, even roses – none of which I have treated as the professionals advise. In fact I almost prefer the well-known varieties of everlasting flower hanging, as above, during their drying process than in conventional arrangements.

I have an enormous dried flower arrangement in my drawing room which was started about ten years ago and I mention it first because it is another illustration of the way I break my own rules.

Generally, dried flower arrangements should not be kept year in and year out, as they tend to lose their appeal through becoming over-familiar and covered in dust. But this arrangement is now about 1.25m (4ft) high by 1m (3ft) wide and I am always adding to it when I see a particularly good allium, or thistle head, or hogweed, or when one of the leaves has to be cut off the banana plant in the hall. Everything goes in fresh and is left to dry in the display and, when the oldest flowers and leaves begin to crumble, they are removed. In this way the arrangement is constantly renewed and altered, and its position is sometimes changed in the room so that it gains a new look.

Most dried flower compositions should be taken apart and regenerated by re-arranging regularly and, in the spring, it is best to store the contents in plastic bags, so that they may be brought out again in the autumn. Dried flowers do not really suit the warmer months when there is plenty of fresh and colourful material around.

Throughout the year I am constantly cutting with drying and winter use in mind. Flowers and leaves must be gathered at just the right time in order to make sure that their colours are preserved as much as possible. For instance, the globe artichoke should be picked when the flower is really blue; most flowers should not be fully open and should certainly not have begun to set seed, otherwise they will simply disintegrate into fluff when dried. However, bells of Ireland (*Moluccella laevis*) must have the flower in the top bract open and hydrangeas should be at the point where their bright early colours are fading into muted shades of pink, green, mauve and blue.

It is important that dried arrangements should contain a mass of ingredients and not be just one or two sticks in the vase. Unless the contents are tightly grouped, they will begin to fall and slacken, but, in any case, they should continually be given body by new additions. But, as always, there are exceptions to all rules and some single varieties can look well.

There are a number of methods of drying flowers and foliage. The most common is to hang bunches upside down in an airy but shady place. If it is too light, the flowers lose a lot of colour and may become brittle and, if it is damp, they are attacked by mildew. They should be free from any moisture and their foliage should be stripped away before they are hung, as these leaves usually shrivel and are useless. The amount of time needed for drying varies; the largest plants taking about three weeks and grasses and delicate flowers only about seven days.

Everlasting flowers are most suited to this method. These are annuals grown in sunny spots especially for preserving. Yellow, pink, orange, red and white *Helichrysum bracteatum* are the best known and should be picked as the petals begin to open and before they are in full bloom. Pink or white daisy type *Helipterum roseum*; silvery white and yellow *Ammobium alatum*; sea lavender (*Statis*), one of the most popular of the immortelles, in white, purple, blue or yellow; batchelor's buttons (*Gomphrena globosa*) in red, white and purple; mauve and white xeranthemum, and anaphalis with its white flower and soft grey leaf all come into this category.

Other flowers which respond surprisingly well to air drying by hanging are delphiniums and their annual cousin, larkspur, both of which I often prefer in this form to fresh. Later in their cycle, these plants may also be dried in this way for useful seedheads.

Many other seedheads can be obtained like this. Those of the iris are wonderful, my favourite variety being *Iris foetidissima* with bright orange seeds. All the onion family (*Allium*) are attractive when they have set their seeds. Globe artichoke heads are impressive and those of their close relations, the cardoons, are even better.

Many experts suggest that, with the exceptions of hydrangeas, achilla and *Moluccella laevis*, it is not a good idea to air-dry flowers upright. However, this is, in fact, the way I preserve most of my plants. I stand them in a vase, or container full of water and, after about six weeks, this has evaporated and all the green in the plants has gone leaving very pretty dried flowers.

Gypsophila reacts splendidly to this treatment. When it is fresh, it has a tiny, white flower with a very brilliant, but very thin silver-green leaf, and it dries to a ravishingly delicate silver-fawn cloud.

Mimosa loses its pollen, of course, then dries into little yellow, scented

The summer colours of the annual Helichrysum bracteatum can be carried through into winter, as they retain a substantial amount when dried. These are probably the best known of the everlasting flowers, and can easily be dried by hanging them upside down in an airy but shaded place, such as a verandah or porch.

balls; alchemilla (lady's mantle) turns into fragile sprays of subdued lime-green. All these look very effective when grouped as individual species, and when used to temper mixed arrangements.

Many seedheads can be gathered already dried; poppies, foxgloves, hollyhocks, parsley, cultivated clematis and old man's beard – both the latter being useful for softening big dried bouquets. Other wild plants in this context are cow parsley, giant hogweed, dock seed spires, the dried white bells left after the bluebells have flowered, dropwort, meadow rue, wild fennel and the hundreds of wild grasses. In summer, it is worth befriending a farmer in order to be able to gather a big container full of ripe barley, oats or wheat. Again, what matters is that these should be concentrated in a solid mass. Sparse whiskers here and there are quite useless. I also use the sunflower's enormous seedheads, which look fabulous, and I like those of *Sedum telephium*, 'Autumn Joy', too.

Foliage is best preserved with a mixture of one part glycerine to two parts hot water. Autumn tinted leaves are not really suitable for this method, as the branches ought to be cut when still full of sap, so that the glycerine mixture will eventually be drawn up and replace the water in the stems.

The branches with their leaves should not be too large. They should

For an Australian client, a professional florist arranged this group of dried seed heads to enhance the collection of objects. In contrast to this full arrangement, two single dried flower heads are placed close by in a small, early pottery container.

be hammered lightly at their bases and then conditioned for a few hours in deep water before treatment begins. They should then be stood in 10cm (4in) of the mixture in cylindrical containers, to keep them upright, and left for about three weeks. Large, individual leaves, such as hostas, magnolia, rhododendron and laurel, may also be preserved like this. The foliage will finally change colour, young leaves growing lighter and mature leaves darker, and become glossy; a number also turn shades of rust and purple.

Eucalyptus is lovely after this treatment; ivy and aspidistra leaves respond well, too, although the latter require several months before they are ready. This is the way to preserve young beech, maple, bay, oak branches with acorns, and choisya.

Another popular method of drying some of the more delicate flowers is by using borax powder, or silver sand. Personally, I prefer borax, as sand is often too heavy for the petals, and this is the treatment which I think preserves the original flower colours best.

Cover the bottom of a box with borax powder and gently lay the flowers in this, then sprinkle more powder until the flowers are completely covered, making sure that it has reached into all their folds and corners. This works very quickly as the borax draws the moisture from the flowers, and they must be extracted at just the right time. Often, this is only a matter of hours later. Small roses take about twelve hours, cornflowers about thirty-six hours and larger blooms about two weeks. Daffodils look superb after this treatment and zinnias, the hellebores, delphiniums, anemones, sunflowers and snowdrops all react well to it.

Silica gel is a variation which involves mixing the crystals with cobalt in proportions of 450g (1lb) of silica gel to 25g (1oz) of cobalt, working this over and round the flowers in a box, then leaving them for about a week. However, some experts find this too heavy for fragile flowers.

There are one or two dried plants which I generally avoid. Chinese lanterns (*Physalis*), honesty, teazles and bullrushes have been used badly so often that now they remind me of dentists' waiting rooms. However, the occasional bullrush in an important dried arrangement may look effective, or a large number of them grouped architecturally. The only way to use honesty is as an absolutely immense

bunch. It must never be small and awkward, so it will not mix. Pampas grass, too, must be handled with care. If the position and size of the room are suitable, you might take twenty plumes, which would look architecturally interesting, but two or three pieces in a big mixed bouquet are acceptable, although this is not a favourite of mine and there are other much more impressive imported varieties of these big grasses.

You should also be careful with driftwood, twisted bark and skeletal branches. Arrangements built round these must not look 'arty-crafty' and, again, this is often a question of scale. You can do a very good architectural arrangement of dead branches, driftwood and twigs, if you are bold. It must be big and meaningful and done with strength in a large pottery container, say 30cm (12in) in diameter by 40cm (16in) deep.

In order to whiten driftwood and branches, they should be soaked in a bleach solution for a day, rubbed down with sandpaper and then left as they are. Never wax them.

Once you stray from the straight forward arrangement in its container, the whole medium of dried plants has to be approached cautiously. An unfortunate number of displays and objects are produced with this material which are remarkable only for their ugliness. Dried arrangements in picture frames, mixtures of dried flowers and plastic fruits, figurines carrying armfuls of dried grasses, and china spoons decorated with glittered dried flowers and satin ribbon are in no way acceptable to me.

However, the Victorian fashion of having little round cushion posies of everlasting flowerheads is delightful. A child's basket filled with dried flowers and leaves may also be pretty and I like very much making dried flowers 'trees'. These may be shaped like Christmas trees and packed solidly with little flowerheads, or with cones and seedheads. The basic shape is cut out of florist's foam or by winding a piece of fine wire netting into a cone shape, which may then be lined with newspaper or foam, and sealed at the foot with hessian over cardboard. Other 'trees' may be built as round heads on bamboo trunks.

An interesting composition is created by stuffing an open wicker or wire wastepaper basket with newspaper, turning it upside down and then covering the whole surface – sides and

top – densely with dried plant material. This does use a very large number of ingredients, but you finish up with a mountain of dried and preserved flowers, fruit, foliage and seedheads.

Dried flowers make pretty and long-lasting gifts, either pre-arranged, or simply as unadorned material for your friends to arrange themselves. My shops all over the world stock the Victorian posies and flower trees I have mentioned and we find them universally popular.

It does take a certain amount of practice and experience to become really successful at drying your own flowers, but it is worthwhile experimenting and preserving, because the end results are so effective and they do add considerably to your sources of material for winter.

Most florists, and even many department stores now stock equipment, such as preserving powders, foam, shapes, wires and so on, which you might need, as well as a wide range of dried plants, both home grown and imported. Sometimes, these flowers are expensive, but remember that, with care, they will last for years and, used imaginatively, should give you a lot of enjoyment. The use of dried plants adds yet another dimension to the pleasant activity of arranging flowers.

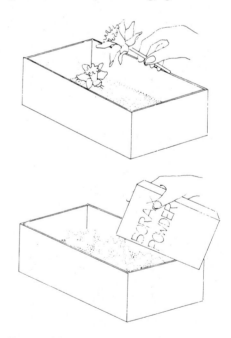

Drying delicate flowers in borax.
Top: Lay the flower heads on a layer of borax powder in a box.
Above: Sprinkle borax over the flowers, making sure it has reached all their folds and corners. Silver sand and silica gel can be used in a similar way, but I find both too heavy for most flowers.

A Dutch client wasted nothing in arranging these two dried giant hogweed stems in an almost Japanese manner, supporting the upright pieces with tightly packed sections of stem. The natural material of the plain varnished basket works well with the texture of the dried plant. Hogweed grows wild, and may often be picked naturally dried.

Simplicity is perhaps the quality to search for most in arrangements, no matter what kind of flower or foliage you are dealing with. Here, everything is from the hedgerows, and has a poetic style about it, reminiscent of the painter Odilon Redon. The wildflowers here include the common dandelion, poppy and cow parsley.

Postscript

*Rosa x 'Apricot Silk' a modern rose,
but with a dazzling orange bloom.*

In the end, there is only one rule which matters. Flowers are for pleasure. Looking at them, handling them and arranging them should always be enjoyable and should not be limited by unnecessary regulations and taboos.

If you like the formal traditions, then by all means do flowers in those ways sometimes, but try not to allow these rather rigid styles to dictate your whole attitude towards flower arranging. Experiment, try out new ideas and break the rules – everyone's rules! I always do.

Instead of worrying about conforming to old restrictions, energy is better expended on planning a year-round supply of plant material for your vases and containers, either from the garden, or, if you live in town, through growing a wide and original range of flowers indoors and on the balcony.

Although I have strong preferences among flowers and foliage, and there are one or two which I hardly entertain at all, my Utopian garden would contain every species of plant, because each does have a part to play.

For instance, although I do not like salvias, I would certainly have them growing in a garden of four square beds with red standard fuchsias in the middle and a purple-leaved plum (*Prunus cistina*) hedge around the edge, to create a build-up of reds and purples. Then, at the end of August, when there are a lot of reds around, the salvias would be used in arrangements.

Dahlias would also be grown, not because I particularly like them, but because they have very, very useful colours at certain stages of the year. There would be a square, hedged-in October garden full of Michaelmas daisies, which remind me of my youth, although I rarely use them indoors.

In fact, nothing would be rejected and the dream garden would, in reality, be many gardens, divided by hedges, as it were into rooms by species and colour.

Every flower arranger probably has a secret dream garden just as I do and, even though it is unattainable, thinking about it makes us re-examine our likes and dislikes and sometimes discover new ways of presenting plants we may previously have despised, as well as those we love.

Visiting famous gardens is an extension of this search for ideas. Seeing what others have achieved out of doors often opens up new indoor themes.

One of my favourite gardens is Vita Sackville-West's and Harold Nicolson's at Sissinghurst Castle. The concept of the White Garden there is easily reflected in a white flower arrangement at home using apple blossom, cow parsley, white lilac and late pheasant's eye narcissi. The White Garden, itself, contains festoons of roses, *Lilium regale*, silvery *Cineraria maritima* and, later in the summer, clouds of gypsophila, white *Veronica virginica alba*, white delphiniums and white eremuri, with a beautiful, silver, willow-leaved pear tree in the centre. All these plants may be used to great effect in arrangements.

There are large gardens with marvellous botanical and horticultural collections, of course, but, from a planting and aesthetic design point of view, I believe they invariably lack the taste of those few small gardens which are the great gardens of today. It is in these gardens that one can often see examples of how to put flowers together.

Shaking off preconceptions and concentrating the mind afresh on all the available material does result in unusual and interesting compositions. Roadside weeds, herbacious perennials and shrubs, dried flowers and bought blooms are the rich sources from which to draw inspiration. Do not think of the most complicated approach; aim for simplicity, because there lies the secret of style.

At my mother's memorial service in the Chelsea Royal Hospital chapel, there was not a single flower. I had nothing but different green leaves and herbs massed in two large containers. I had never seen this done in a church before, but it expressed our feelings simply and looked very, very beautiful.

Generally I believe that flower arranging should be light and pleasing. Once it becomes competitive and serious, something to spend sleepless nights over, its magic is lost and this magic is surely its principal attraction. The fragility of the flower and foliage material, the delicate touch required, the moments of exciting discovery, the delight with the finished composition, should all combine to remove us from the stresses and worries of our every day lives and turn this into the most enchanting of pleasures in a tormented, plasticized and pressured world.

INDEX OF PLANTS AND FLOWERS

Cover Design: Eddy Pitcher
Design: Pedro Prá-Lopez   Illustrations: Gwen Simpson
Pictures supplied by:
D. Arminson: 43(1), 48, 61(t), 62; P. Ayres: 17 (lower centre); A-Z
Botanical Collection: 46(b), 57; Barnabys: 4, 50, 66; R. Benfield:79(b);
S. Bicknell: 15, 35, 55, 80; M. Boys: 6, 7, 14, 27, 30, 31, 37, 69, 75;
M. Boys/S. Griggs Agency: 54; J. Burras: 9(r); Camera Press: 56(t);
Camera Press: 56(t); Heidede Carstensen/Jacques Hartz: 77; R. J.
Corbin: 40(b), 43(r); E. Crowson: 17 (upper centre), (bl); A. Denney:
45(1); A. Duns: 56(b); V. Finnis: 13(b), 17 (upper left), (bc),19(r),42(1),
52(r); M. Holford: 61(b); Courtesy Sergeant-at-Arms House of Lords/
Photo Freeman: 70; P. Hunt: 45(r); G. Hyde: 9(c); L. Johns: 12;

J. Ledger: 53; C. Lewis: 49, 64, 74; J. Markham: 67(b); P. Matthews:
17(tr), (lower right), 71; E. Megson: 63(1); R. Rutter: 46(t); Sale,Stone
& Senior: 63(r); M. Slingsby: 76; D. Smith: 40(t); H. Smith: 8, 9(1),
17(tc), (upper right), (lower left), (br), 39, 41(1), 51, 52(1), (c), 79(t), 82;
C. Watmough: 87; M. Wickham: 10, 13(t), 19(b), 29, 59, 81; D.
Woodland: 17(tl), 42(r), 67(t); Zefa: 41(r).

Reprinted from 'David Hicks on Decoration – 5' by kind permission
of Britwell Books: 11, 18, 20, 25, 33, 36, 38, 47, 60, 73, 78, 83, 85, 86.
Reprinted from 'David Hicks on Decoration – with fabrics' by kind
permission of Britwell Books: Frontispiece, 3, 68.